YOU ARE ALWAYS **ONE DECISION** AWAY
FROM A TOTALLY DIFFERENT LIFE

DECISION
AWAY

Published in Canada, for Global Distribution by YGTMedia Co.

www.ygtmedia.co

For more information email: publishing@ygtmedia.co

ISBN trade paperback: 978-1-998754-39-7
eBook: 978-1-998754-40-3

To order additional copies of this book:
publishing@ygtmedia.co

YOU ARE ALWAYS **ONE DECISION** AWAY
FROM A TOTALLY DIFFERENT LIFE

One

DECISION
AWAY

AMANDA WILSON-CIOCCI

AMANDA JEROME . JESSICA FLYNN . CAITLIN NAGY . JODIE HEFFREN
AMANDA LEPIANE . LORI BERENZ . JULIA WALSH . EDIE GUDAITIS
NONA MORROW . VANESSA LOCICERO . KIANNA SUNSHINE

TABLE OF *contents*

*You are always one decision away from a
totally different life. And it's never ONE thing . . .
it's the many signs and synchronicities that you
finally see and listen to that inspire you to make the
ONE decision that will impact everything else.*

–AMANDA WILSON–CIOCCI

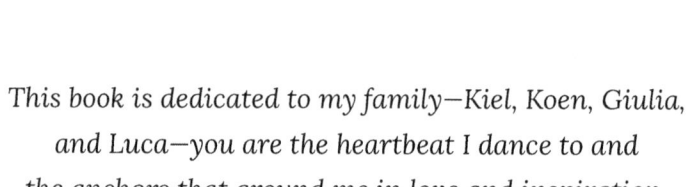

This book is dedicated to my family—Kiel, Koen, Giulia, and Luca—you are the heartbeat I dance to and the anchors that ground me in love and inspiration.

To the coauthors, your "Heck, yes!" that echoes through the pages of this transformative book has added to the tapestry of inspiration and empowerment, and your decision to share your voices and experiences will undoubtedly resonate with countless hearts, sparking courage, expansion, and change.

To the Monarch Community, you are the momentum of this movement. Your passion, authenticity, and commitment to growth inspire me daily, and I am honored to do this work, hold this space, and light up the world with you!

AMANDA WILSON-CIOCCI

Amanda Wilson-Ciocci is the owner of The Monarch & Co., community builder and cocoon maker for women entrepreneurs inside Monarch Momentum, program creator of Monarch Business Academy, best-selling author of *The Monarch*, and lead author of *One Decision Away*. With over twenty years' experience, she helps heart-centered entrepreneurs tap into their authentic stories, passions, and purpose so they can increase their impact, leverage their leadership, launch with clarity, and build legacy with the work they are doing in this world.

@THEMONARCHANDCO
WWW.THEMONARCHANDCO.COM

introduction

YOU ARE ALWAYS ONE DECISION AWAY FROM A TOTALLY DIFFERENT LIFE.

Bold statement, I know. But when I embarked on my journey of entrepreneurship and hit burnout a year in, I read one book that gave me the clarity I needed in order to know what my next steps were going to be, and as a result of that one decision, you are now reading this book.

The book was *If Women Rose Rooted* by Sharon Blackie. Inside the pages, Sharon invites you to "step off the edge" of transformation and "let yourself fall"—and it was these words found buried in the pages that sparked something inside of me:

"Don't fear the dark: it's a natural part of the Journey. The most beautiful butterflies emerge from the darkness of the cocoon... Out of the darkness comes strength, and focus."

When I was twenty-two years old, I was diagnosed with thyroid cancer. About two weeks after surgery to remove the butterfly-shaped gland from my neck, I sat healing in my basement apartment. I remember looking up at the small window from my bed thinking the light seemed so far away. It felt like I was in a deep dark hole, and regardless of how loud I yelled or how far I stretched out my hand in hopes of someone grabbing it and pulling me out, I was alone. And worse than being alone, the light felt out of reach. In paralyzing fear of my physical and mental state, I sat in the stillness and listened. In the distance, I heard a voice, and as I lay there, it got louder and said: You are the only one who can get yourself out of here.

In that moment, I healed my spirit and realized my power. I didn't need someone to save me and pull me from the dark hole—I had everything I needed inside of me. "A pilgrimage begins with one small step." I knew the journey ahead of me wasn't going to be easy, but I was ready to embrace it, welcome the twists and turns, and LIVE.

I'm a survivor, not a quitter. I don't give up or give in. I am stronger than I think. I am brave, fierce, and I am here. I have gratitude for my journey and clarity on my purpose and mission in this world. The golden thread that has woven my tapestry is now part of yours. You are here for a reason. These words were meant for your eyes and your heart. And for that, I am both excited for you and honored to be part of your journey.

After reading that one book with the words that so deeply resonated with my soul, I listened to the whispers and went on to launch Monarch Business Academy, my signature program and transformative experience to help women entrepreneurs build and launch their signature programs and services out in the world. I published a book in hopes that the words inside the cover would ignite a spark and create a butterfly effect, helping inspire entrepreneurs on their journey—and it did, becoming a bestseller! On Women's Day in 2023, I opened a membership community for heart-centered women entrepreneurs to find a safe space to land, gain inspiration and clarity on their gifts, and connect and collaborate in community so they could continue putting one foot in front of the other to gain momentum in their life and business and not have to do it alone.

The coauthors in this book are all Monarchs. They have journeyed through Monarch Business Academy (MBA) to gain clarity on their purpose and next steps, to connect with other women on heart-centered missions, and to be safe in a cocoon so they could spread their wings, fly, and do what they are meant to do in this world. These women said yes to themselves, their big visions, and listened to the voice that got louder. And it's in the pages of this book where you will discover the golden thread that connects us all together in this tapestry of life.

A NOTE TO
THE READER

It's never ONE thing. It's not one book, one decision, one mentor, one course, one anything that changes the trajectory of your life. It is the many decisions, the many signs and synchronicities that you finally see and listen to that inspire you to make the ONE decision that will impact everything else.

You may read this book from cover to cover or flutter around through different pages, stories, and chapters. Regardless of where you land, this book was created for you to stop in interesting places and find inspiration and opportunities for personal growth along the way.

The stories in this book will make you laugh, cry, feel inspired and connected. The themes in these stories speak to the power of mindset, resiliency, adaptability, fear, joy, courage, and power. Together, we will embark on a journey to explore the transformative power of decisions and the boundless potential that lies within each of us. Within these chapters, we aim to serve as catalysts for change and sources of motivation. Our intention is to demonstrate how a single decision can have a profound impact, leading us down unexpected paths and opening doors we never knew existed. But let us not be confined by the notion of one pivotal decision alone. Life is a tapestry woven with countless choices and golden threads, both significant and seemingly insignificant, that shape our experiences and determine our outcomes.

In this book, we invite you to reflect upon the power within you and to move forward with purpose and intention. It is not merely in the decisions themselves but also in your ability to embrace them, to trust your intuition, and to listen to your inner voice and gut feelings even (or especially) when those voices seem to go against the grain. We want to empower you to take ownership of your unique power and acknowledge the potential for growth that lies within each decision, big or small.

As you dive into the chapters ahead, we encourage you to approach them as sources of inspiration, realizing that the stories we share are meant to spark your own inner transformation. Allow them to ignite the flame of possibility within you and guide you toward your own extraordinary journey. Remember, the power resides not solely in one decision but in the multitude of choices you make every day.

Together, let us embrace the infinite potential that lies within us and embark on a path of self-discovery, growth, and empowerment. Our collective stories will illuminate the interconnectedness of our journeys, and through our shared experiences, we will uncover the beauty and significance of every decision we make—for within these pages, we discover that our potential knows no bounds.

All too often we find ourselves caught in the trap of deferring our dreams and aspirations to some elusive future. However, the truth remains that the future is built upon the choices we make today . . .

—JESSICA FLYNN

THE TRUTH REMAINS
THAT THE FUTURE IS BUILT
UPON THE CHOICES WE
MAKE TODAY.

To Greg, Hunter, Vienna, Mom, and Dad. Your unwavering love, constant encouragement, and boundless patience have been instrumental in shaping me into the woman you have always believed me to be. Your support has been the foundation upon which I have built this beautiful life, and for that, I am eternally grateful.

JESSICA FLYNN

Jessica Flynn is a serial entrepreneur who currently lives on the shores of Georgian Bay with her soulmate Greg, son Hunter, and daughter Vienna. She's the founder and CEO of The You Power Project, a for-profit social enterprise delivering youth programs designed to build confidence, resiliency, and transferable skills through the exploration of entrepreneurship. She's also the CEO of a small business consultancy, The Flynn Collaboration, providing high-level support to business owners on an as-needed basis. During the writing of this chapter, she resigned from a thirteen-year teaching career, landed in TD Canada's Top 100 Mom-Entrepreneurs, and was selected as a recipient of the Education 2.0 Conference Outstanding Leadership Award.

@THEYOUPOWERPROJECT
@JESSICA_FLYNNER

CHAPTER 1:
YOU'LL NEVER FEEL
COMPLETELY READY

Someone asked me once, "Why can't you just be happy with what you have?" I was thirty-one years old and seemed to have it all: the full-time teaching job, the house, the spouse, a baby on the way. I was on track to have the life I'm sure you've already been able to conjure up in your head. Yet despite having achieved these societal markers of success, I found myself in a constant state of restlessness, of yearning for something more. The moment I was asked this question reinforced for me that I had different measures of success, of finding fulfillment. But I also felt guilty about not wanting what everyone else around me seemed to want.

My parents both had successful careers climbing the ladder, so to speak. I saw their formula for success, and it made sense. At the age of twenty-three, I moved to Collingwood, Ontario, to pursue the teaching career I thought I wanted, in a geographic landscape that truly drew me in. At the time I had no idea it would take me eight years to land a permanent job with the board that had just hired me, but I have to say, I made very productive use of those eight years.

During that time I met my husband, an entrepreneur, as well as his equally enterprising parents. I found myself in uncharted territory. The meaning of the word "entrepreneur" was unfamiliar to me, but the vibrant energy and relentless pursuit of a fulfilling life that radiated from them was instantly captivating. Their approach to success was both exhilarating and refreshingly fun and creative, opening my eyes to a whole new world of possibilities. While playing the supply / short-term-teaching contract game, I became the education director for the new Oxford Learning Centre in town, had my first business mentor, and was given the opportunity to manage and lead a team of educators. With one foot in the school system and one foot out exploring, I continued to volunteer in the community, networking wherever I went, and diversifying my skill set, while often being made to feel like I was "bouncing around" professionally. Next, I was offered the opportunity to become the operations manager of a new resort spa. While sponging up everything I could from my next set of mentors and leading a team of more than forty wellness practitioners, I, along with my husband, had also been managing my husband's rental properties and renovating a 150-year-old home in the heart of town. Throughout those years, I tried to balance my teaching career by taking on limited long-term-occasion contracts alongside my burgeoning businesses.

After three years of renos, a magazine feature of our project, and loads of creative energy, I left the spa to launch my first solo business, Funky Bunkies—a boutique construction company niching in small structures. Our success was uncanny, and I wasn't ready for it. I was thirty, designing, quoting, project managing, managing trades on multiple sites for high-end clients, and pregnant with our first child. I needed to scale but had no idea how to do it. Then, after nearly eight years, my name finally floated to the top of the list. The permanent teaching job. With an uncertain path forward in the business and a baby on the way, I took the job and silenced that pesky entrepreneurial spirit of mine. Or so I thought.

Lessons from a Disney Princess

Inspiration can come from unexpected places. Insert my fave Disney flick, *Frozen II*. (FYI, I'm not a Disney fan girl. I will never adorn a Mickey Mouse tattoo, and my intolerance for crowds will likely keep us from ever visiting in person; however, I am nerdy for the Frozen franchise.)

Frozen II begins with Elsa, having overcome heart-wrenching loss and a profound identity crisis in the original film, now living happily with her sister and their makeshift little family. On the surface, it appears that the heroine has found her place in the world. She's living her "truth," using her gifts for the betterment of others, and fulfilling her destiny as the leader of her people. From an outsider's perspective, what more could she possibly want?

But then she hears a voice, a calling that beckons her to venture into the unknown and connect with her deepest, most authentic self. I found myself belting out those lyrics in the car, resonating with her internal struggle to ignore the whispers pushing her to follow a new path. Despite making a difference in her community and utilizing her gifts, she realizes that her unique powers have outgrown her current environment. She senses that there is more to her existence beyond the confines of her current role. I made a personal connection to the struggles of this animated ice queen.

You see, I am a natural-born educator, yet from the moment I was accepted into teacher's college, I knew deep down that the traditional classroom wasn't where I belonged. And I was right. I felt trapped, confined, and limited, as if I could only express a fraction of my true self. Teaching was only one of my many talents. For me, the conventional classroom mirrored the castle—a place where I knew I could never fully live out my true destiny.

I used my second maternity leave to dabble some more. I enrolled in several online business courses and coaching pro- grams. During the pandemic, I launched my first virtual youth program, Be Your Own B.O.S.S.™, and at the same time, I also began offering free consulting to my business-owner pals.

While trapped in a windowless office cubby, I used to day- dream about how I wanted to spend my days. Now, as the owner of several businesses, my days are filled with more creativity and fulfillment than I could have imagined. I work 1:1 with clients to help them achieve their goals, provide group youth coaching, and create programs focused on youth entrepreneurship and skills-building. I pitch to investors and sponsors, collaborate on community projects, serve on committees, invest in real estate, and carry out swoon-worthy renovations. I meet with developers to imagine sustainable communities in our area, attend retreats and workshops led by my brilliant peers, speak at business events, and spend leisurely days at the family cottage. I have the flexibility to be available for school bus pickups, soccer games and playdates, and I'm looking forward to weekday kayaking adventures with my husband from the beach in our backyard.

I sprang into action my vision to create a better world and a more fulfilling life for myself. Now, proudly taking on the title of "serial entrepreneur" feels like being free every day. It allows all aspects of who I am to shine. It's when the answers to "what do you do for a living" and "how would you describe yourself" align perfectly.

In two years I haven't taken on a project that I'm not obsessed with. At the time of writing this chapter, I submitted my formal resignation to my school board. Do I have every day over the next ten years mapped out? No. But I DO know they will be BRIGHT AF. I am giddy to see what opportunities flood in now that I have sent a sonic boom message saying "This is the life I'm choosing! I am ready! This is me!"

Embracing the title of "Entrepreneur" as part of my identity has unlocked a wellspring of creativity and expanded my ability to make a meaningful impact. It has also allowed for serendipitous moments of magic. However, reaching this point has been a journey. I had to learn how to listen to my intuition and cultivate a growth mindset that supports me, even during the most challenging moments.

FEAR (will you Fear Everything And Run OR Face Everything And Rise?)

We are all scared. At some point or another we (myself included) all think we don't have the skills or the know-how to pull off what we want to.

Back in university, for three of my four years in my theater degree, I was too scared to audition for anything. Finally, I gathered enough courage (and encouragement) to audition for THE major production of the year: a tragedy of all things (not the bright and cheery musicals I used to star in back in high school). In the audition, I was given the direction to "do the whole monologue again, but this time, fill the space." I had NO idea what the director meant. So I took a deep breath and did my Lady Macbeth monologue with bigger hand gestures and wider eyes, and I walked around the stage floor in a giant circle. And it worked! I landed the leading role. In that moment, here's what I learned:

- You deserve to take up space, so literally take up space! You will make a bigger impact.
- Do things that make you scared. You'll be surprised by how you rise to the challenge.
- Make it up. You may think you're in the dark, but as it turns out, most of us are making it up! You will never feel ready for a decision that could change your life.

And know that we all fear failure and the pressure. NBA basketball coach Doc Rivers says, "Pressure is a privilege." To be in a position where you could see a significant advance in your career and in your life means you've gotten to that spot where you have this opportunity. You have your health. You have your family or whatever it is that got you there.

I would have never been ready to become a mom. I did it scared. BUT! I did it supported. And I did it with a deep knowing that motherhood was my destiny.

Listen, I'm not saying taking risks is a comfortable feeling. The unfamiliar may be daunting, but sometimes the known scares me even more. Sure, there are moments of fear and stress when uncertainty looms, but the known is truly terrifying to me in some cases. It's because we know the outcome if we remain stagnant, if we refuse to change. I vividly recall a Jim Rohn quote on my daily desk calendar: "If you don't like where you are, move! You're not a tree." That quote pushed me to launch my first business within a month of reading it (and the quote still hangs on my bulletin board).

Considering a teaching career where I would know what each day for the next three decades would entail (including the financial aspect) made me incredibly uneasy. I know for many people, this knowing offers the opposite effect. Where are you on that scale? As an entrepreneur, some months I earn less than my steady teaching salary. Yet in just a couple years, I am consistently hitting months when I make more than double that salary (and all on my own time). I'm far more confident betting on myself than relinquishing control to others. If I were gone tomorrow, I know I would have fewer regrets than if I had settled.

All too often we find ourselves caught in the trap of deferring our dreams and aspirations to some elusive future. However, the truth remains that the future is built upon the choices we make today. Our world is the result of people pushing past that fear, making the decision to better themselves and their communities. It's how we have everything we have now!

Step into your power. Be the B.O.S.S. of your life.

The You Power Project™ is my for-profit social enterprise offering virtual empowerment programs and coaching to youth ages twelve to twenty-nine. We promise to build confidence, resiliency, and transferable skills through the exploration of entrepreneurship (because honestly, despite all my formal education, entrepreneurship has been my most expansive learning journey). Our flagship program is built around the B.O.S.S. framework™, which stands for Believe anything's possible, Own that anything's possible for you, Shape your ideas into opportunities, and Share your ideas with the world!

I found my formula for finding empowerment in entrepreneurship. At The You Power Project, we celebrate our students' uniqueness and then create ACTION plans to better their own lives and the lives of those in their communities. And let me tell you, these youth have some powerful ideas! They are more connected to their creative genius than most adults. For us, empowerment is found through encouraging words, a supportive community, and REALIZED ACTION. It's learning new skills; it's shining your light into the work you do; it's taking up space.

In the becoming of my current (confident, resilient, and creative) self, there were a number of exercises I worked through (and continue to work through) that accelerated my expansion. If you're feeling like you're ready to explore the next level of YOU (entrepreneurial or otherwise), here are the top three exercises I recommend you activate:

1) Create a vision board. This ignited my own journey toward my dream life. Never made one before? Use those Audible credits and download *The Source* by Dr. Tara Swart to get into the proper mindset. Next, gather scissors, paper, and magazines that inspire you. Allow yourself the luxury of time as you curate images, words, and symbols that represent your deepest desires and aspirations. Let your daydreams become real and embrace the possibility of achieving them. Invest in a beautiful frame and find the perfect spot on the wall where you'll see it every day. Look at your vision board and visualize your future self living that dream life. Feel the excitement, joy, and fulfillment that it brings. But don't stop there. Take a closer look and assess the gaps between your current reality and that envisioned future. Identify the steps and actions you need to take today to bridge those gaps. Break it down into manageable tasks and commit to making progress, no matter how small, each day.

2) Learn your human design. Hop on YouTube or download a great human design (HD) app like Jenna Zoe's. Of all my education and entrepreneurial prep, learning my HD, then receiving coaching on how to step into my genius zone, has been THE most important learning in my life to date.

3) Hear it from someone else. Write down the names of the people who know you best (limit it to three people max) and ask them these questions:

"What are my two greatest strengths?"
"If I had my own show, what would it be about?"
"What do you see me doing ten years from now?"
"What do you think I'm good at that I don't recognize about myself yet?"

"When do I tend to get sad, angry, and frustrated the most?"

"How would you describe me to a stranger?"

Don't be so afraid that you silence your soul. Listen to those around you who see your gifts, who see your strengths, and who see the vision of your brightest future, even when you can't. And then you must ACT.

Consider your twelve-year-old self

What did twelve-year-old you KNOW was possible? What were your hopes and dreams? In our youth programs, I meet many twelve-year-olds, and more times than not, they are incredibly perceptive and self-aware. They possess a unique blend of childhood innocence and future-oriented thinking. They recognize their strengths, yearnings, hopes, and abilities with remarkable clarity.

Amid the chaos and demands of the world around us, it's easy to lose touch with our purpose and our humanity. That's why it's crucial to reconnect with what you knew about yourself when you were twelve because those truths still resonate within you. The strength, the knowing, and the vision of what you could achieve are all still present. If you find yourself falling short of the potential your young and optimistic self saw for you, consider what decision you can make today that would make them proud.

Remember, too, that twelve-year-old version of you had a specific context in mind when envisioning who you would become. To unleash my creativity and occupy the space I knew I was meant for, I initially thought I would become an actress or a pop star. However, in my current work, I get to be creative, share my voice, stand on stages, and make a meaningful impact. I am living the life my younger self hoped for and more. I believe that Jessica from 1999 would definitely be proud of where I am and excited to see what else I can accomplish.

Are you just one decision away from an entirely different career and life? Can you become a more authentic version of yourself, the person your twelve-year-old self always knew you would be? If you don't begin to make moves toward your goals, then when will they become realized? How will they materialize?

For me, the most important decision was to leave behind the environment I thought I should want in order to fully step into my most authentic, holistic self. Like Elsa trading her gig at the castle for her true calling out in the Enchanted Forest. You were once a little kid with big dreams that you promised you'd make real one day. Don't disappoint them. Begin taking even the tiniest steps toward your deepest dreams and desires and watch them materialize. Your younger self believed in you and knew you had the potential to achieve greatness. Don't let them down. Embrace your true calling, unleash your creativity, and become the version of yourself that you were meant to be.

In the end, it's not about the external measures of success like fame or fortune. It's about living a life that aligns with your passions, values, and purpose. It's about making a positive impact and leaving a lasting legacy.

Create your vision board. The time to live your dreams is now. Seize it.

The thing I didn't know way back then, or in the many years that followed, is that there are two ways to make a decision: one is based on what's easy, and one is based on what's hard. The easy way usually doesn't get you what you really need long term. It gets you quick fixes. The hard way, as it turns out, isn't actually all that hard, but you have to dig really deep to figure it out.

—JULIA WALSH

NO MATTER HOW TIRED I AM OR
HOW HECTIC LIFE IS, IT'S UP TO ME
TO MOVE MYSELF FORWARD.

To my mum, who really and truly and sometimes annoyingly is always right. To my husband, for encouraging me to figure out what really does light me up. To my career-coaching childhood bestie who set me on the right path. And to my daughters, Zoë and Sloan, for inspiring me to give them the best version of myself.

JULIA WALSH

Julia Walsh is the creative genius behind J Walsh Social Co., a boutique digital marketing agency, who most commonly answers to "Jules" or "Mum"—she's got many names and talents! For the past five years, Julia has been honing her skills at amplifying the intersection of branding and social media. With her supercharged communication skills and passion for building relationships (and new friendships), she's busy connecting clients with their ideal audiences. Armed with proven strategies and artistic creativity, she has a solid record of helping brands stand out online. When she's not working with clients, Julia hangs out in Barrie, Ontario, with her husband, two adorable daughters, and their crazy Boston Terrier.

@JWALSHSOCIAL

CHAPTER 2:
SOMETIMES THE EASIEST
CHOICE IS THE HARDEST

I never knew what I wanted to be when I grew up. According to my mum, however, when I was three, I wanted to be Mr. T. But aside from that, I never had much clarity. I used to be envious of friends who always knew what their passion was. I remember when I was seven, my friend told me she wanted to be a cardiologist. I said "cool," and we continued playing with Barbies. Here we are, thirty-plus years later, and she is an amazing and well-respected general surgeon. She had clarity, dedication, and a badass surgeon type of personality from the age of seven. My personality made me quip "I pity the fool!" and laugh heartily, but I didn't end up being Mr. T.

The thing I didn't know way back then, or in the many years that followed, is that there are two ways to make a decision: one is based on what's easy, and one is based on what's hard. The easy way usually doesn't get you what you really need long term. It gets you quick fixes. The hard way, as it turns out, isn't actually all that hard, but you have to dig really deep to figure it out.

Guess which way I made most of my decisions during my early career years? You guessed it! The easy way.

Case in point: I applied to university for English because I loved reading. I had no clue what I was going to do with the degree.

The path to being Mr. T was not in earning a degree in English, but what did I care?

After graduation, I got a job working for a pharmaceutical software company in the States through the magic of nepotism. It was cool that I got to move to Philadelphia and travel, but the job? Meh. There was no passion, and it didn't challenge me. I thought, *Maybe this is the thing. The thing that I will one day love. Or maybe it's all a lie that you can love your job, and I'll just keep showing up and keep getting paid. That's cool too.*

Spoiler alert: It wasn't cool.

Four years later I woke up more homesick than usual and realized that even though I didn't know what I wanted, I knew it wasn't that job. So I packed up my bags and headed back home. My small Canadian town welcomed me with open arms. I took random jobs in retail and hospitality and trucked my way through my midtwenties, all while wondering when I'd figure life out. I eventually moved to Toronto, signed on with a temp agency, then found myself once again sitting at a desk and staring at computer screens.

Definitely not for me. Time to make a change. I felt like I had to make a big-impact decision that would guide me into the rest of my life, I just didn't know what or how to make it.

Why isn't success easy?

Other people's success always looks easy, doesn't it? We look at them and think, *Hey! Why did that work for you, but not me? How did you get that job and then get promoted?* People around me were thriving in their careers. To me, it looked like they had well-designed plans and were purposefully moving forward. Of course, I know now that wasn't the case for many of them. Some people fell into things; some people struggled. At that point in our lives we rarely talked about it, though.

An interesting fact, however, is that many of my friends were in jobs and careers that had nothing to do with what they went to school for. So it wasn't just me! I kept hearing the line, "Find what brings you joy and get paid for that." Okay, but reading fiction and doing crafts while drinking wine didn't seem to be hiring. Definitely time for that big-impact decision.

Except I made the next decision the easy way. My friend applied to go back to school for interior design. It sparked my interest, so I decided to apply as well. It sounded fun! I envisioned a future career where I owned my own design firm and created all the beautiful spaces.

But that's not where it led me. I graduated and landed at an educational institution in its furnishings department. The job was fine. There wasn't anything terrible about it. But it wasn't the exciting kind of career I had imagined. Lots of sitting at a desk and staring at a screen. Retrospectively, I can say that my personal life at that time was flourishing while I was there. I spent amazing time with friends, I got married, and I had my babies, all while working there. Perhaps the stability of the job was what I needed right then.

Life changes things, though, doesn't it? Changing from single to married to parenthood shifted things. Before these changes it was enough to just be doing the job that was okay with that niggling feeling that it wasn't right because I felt like I still had years to figure it out, whatever "it" was. But motherhood gave me different priorities, and I felt like I had a screaming banshee telling me that I needed to change NOW. I was exhausted from commuting and seeing my children for just a couple hours a day for a job I didn't really love. I was honestly depressed at the notion that this would be my life for the next few decades.

So, back to the decisions. Clearly, my previous approach wasn't the best. It was time to go the hard way. Remember that I said that the "hard way" wasn't actually all that hard? It's true!

So here it is. The one decision that changed my life. I decided to listen to myself. I decided I deserve a life that honors who I am.

How did I do that? It started with career counseling. At first, I was hesitant. I mean, I thought, *What kind of idiot needs therapy for their job?* Turns out, this kind of idiot. My experiences thus far in life had shown me that nothing was a right fit for me, and I didn't know if it was me, or if it was the kinds of jobs I was picking. I was tired of trying to fit into boxes just because they were there. I had the personal desire and the support from my family to really make an investment in both time and money to see what I could figure out.

Luckily, my childhood best friend was a career coach, and I knew she'd be kind and patient with me. And I trusted her to be able to talk about my fears and be vulnerable about my past.

The importance of values

The things I learned while working with her were not rocket science. In fact, I kind of already knew deep down a lot of the things we talked about, but I didn't actually realize that they applied to making decisions in my career, like how important it is to align your values with the work you do. So, I reflected on my values. I explored the disconnect to them. I envisioned what my career and my life could be like if I honored them. And I started researching different career paths that would actually align with my values. I soon began seeing that I would be happier if I had the flexibility to work from home and create a better work–life balance. The daily commute that had me out of the house and away from my family from 6 a.m. to 6 p.m. was draining me. I wanted a work-from-home job, but this was pre-COVID, so it wasn't like those opportunities were abundant.

I did a lot of work to understand what I was interested in, what motivated me, what filled my cup, and what excited me. Being around people, helping, laughing, communicating—those things filled me up. Meeting new people, hearing their stories . . . that inspired me. I married those interests with my values and with opportunity and landed somewhere exciting yet scary. Social media management. On my own. As a small business. It was a complete 180-degree pivot, and I was ready for it. For the first time I felt like I was making the right decision backed up by solid reasoning. So I left my job, and I started my own business.

My passion for this new job grew daily. I was creating the work–life balance I so desired. I was a present parent. I was excited about my work and actually making money with my business!

Of course, I'm sure I don't have to tell you that actual work–life balance is a constant effort. Just when you think you've got a good flow going, life tilts, the pendulum swings, and everything feels chaotic. And then it's calm again. Then you run out of milk, your kid barfs on you, you realize you forgot to email that client back, and you want to cry. But then it all settles down and you're the queen of your world again. I've come to realize that it's not really a balancing act at all; it's more like harmony—making all the things work together in a way that allows for fluctuation and forgiveness. It's perfectly imperfect, and it's different for everyone.

I won't lie to you, though. The business I was building sometimes felt like it was too much, and I doubted myself (I still do, and I think that's only human). I was so disorganized and scattered and had serious bouts of no drive. Then there was a day when I felt like I was drowning in it all, so I reminded myself to just listen. What did I hear?

I heard the doctor diagnosing my daughter with ADHD. I thought about the challenges and struggles she had and the improvements we've seen in her since we started meeting her needs differently. I thought, *You know, I'm kind of the same as her.* Now, I am aware to not Google-diagnose myself, but I couldn't resist. The more I thought about it, the more it made sense. Memes I had laughed at for ages with "OMG that's so me!" suddenly took a whole new meaning because they were true! I met with my doctor, we did some tests, and it turns out that yup, I've got ADHD.

Time to freak out?

Not really.

It was more like a giant sigh of relief. It helped me realize that my brain just works differently than others and I'm not, in fact, a lazy, hot mess. Do you know that ADHD is frequently missed in girls because it presents differently than in boys? Yeah, that's cool.

I've been working with my doctor and my family on adapting to this diagnosis. Nothing changed overnight. It's taken time and a lot of work. The really powerful part about this new understanding of self is that it feels so very freeing. I'm not judging myself so harshly anymore. And I feel seen! It's shocking the number of women I've met who are over forty that are talking to their doctors and being diagnosed with adult ADHD (so many of them are entrepreneurs as well!). It's kind of like life has finally allowed us to listen and ask ourselves why we are the way we are.

Why am I choosing to tell you about my experiences with career coaching and an ADHD diagnosis? Because for years I had felt like there was something wrong with me. I struggled to understand why things always felt so hard. These two moments where I decided to stop and listen to myself were like me actually being Mr. T: strong and cool and empowered.

It took me years of frustration before I realized I could take ownership of my career and eventually, my business. I was frustrated by jobs that just didn't seem to fit. I was frustrated at my performance in my very own business that I loved.

I don't want you to be frustrated. I want you to make that one decision that will set you on the right path. My mum has a saying, one that I remind myself of often: "If you want things to be different, you have to make a change." She's right. She's always right. (Psst, Mum, it's true! You are always right!)

Here's the thing, though. In all of this I have come to realize that no one is going to fix things for me. No one is going to sit me down and ask me the right questions to get the right answer to provide the right solution. No matter how tired I am or how hectic life is, it's up to me to move myself forward.

I'm in a place now where I remember to listen to myself more often. For the first time in a decade, my priority is me. I'm putting myself first. I'm saying yes to opportunities that excite me, I'm saying no to things that don't move me forward professionally, and I'm taking care of myself. Being an entrepreneur feels like a constant uphill battle, and being a mother and an entrepreneur feels like that hill is a mountain. But I'm doing it. And I'm doing it with more confidence and grace now than I could have in my twenties when I wasn't listening to myself. I'm being someone who I can be proud of and who my daughters can be proud of.

You are so much more than you think you are. You are perfect just the way you are. I pity the fool who doesn't know that.

I had to make a choice. I couldn't keep doing it all, and the pandemic taught me that a salary isn't guaranteed. So this time, I chose myself.

–KIANNA SUNSHINE

LIVE BY DESIGN,
NOT BY DEFAULT.

To all the trailblazers.
And most of all, to my hero: my mom.

KIANNA SUNSHINE

Kianna Sunshine is a photographer and writer who empowers women to amplify their awesome to the world. After several successful years working in business, from marketing to public relations, she finally followed her passion for photography and built a thriving business where she draws on her marketing know-how and creativity to inspire and elevate the community.

@KIANNA.SUNSHINE.PHOTOGRAPHY

CHAPTER 3:
THE PRESSURE OF PERFECT

At fifteen, I was hospitalized for my mental health. At twenty-five, I started my own business, tripled my salary, and bought a home. A lot can change in ten years. But here's the secret: it's not your circumstances that have to change, it's your mindset. Once you can shift your thoughts, your outer world shifts with you.

For most of my life I lived in default mode—playing it safe, doing what I was told, and following the clear path that made sense. At the time I thought that faking it until you make it, masking your emotions, and pretending to be someone you're not was the answer. On paper, I was thriving. Internally, I was struggling. But at least everyone saw success, and that was more important than being happy.

Here's a little insight into where my mindset was before I could lean into a life of abundance.

I was born with a heavy expectation: don't fuck up. I believed I had to work twice as hard as everyone else and have a Rolodex of accomplishments to prove something. You see, my mom had me at nineteen. That may not be a big deal today, but in a strict religious community in the nineties, there was a lot of shame, gossip, and judgment.

The environment that nurtured me wasn't very nurturing. I had one shining beacon that always pointed me in the right direction: my rebellious, intelligent, and inspiring mom. She was told she had thrown her life away. She was warned she wouldn't amount to much without a man. An elder in the church told her I'd end up just like her: a teen mom without a future. At the writing of this chapter, my mom is three weeks away from opening her own law firm.

There are many versions of success

Meeting my mom today, you wouldn't know that at age eighteen she hadn't completed high school and was about to tell her parents that her entire world was going to change. Watching her trajectory, I knew I had big shoes to fill. Success was the only option for me. But I didn't realize that there are so many versions of success. Unless you find the version that's meant for you, you might end up miserable.

Have you ever wanted to be something or try something extraordinary but were scared of failing? That was me. I'm here to tell you that despite where you started, your fuckups, and the path you've taken, you're one decision away from an epic life. I just had the most monumental week of my career—becoming a published photographer, receiving a grant to expand my business, and submitting the chapter that will add published author to my bio.

However, growing up, I had no idea what career I wanted. One day it was a doctor. Then maybe on Tuesday, a watchmaker. Actress definitely made the list, as did writer, photographer, TV producer, and more.

I knew my clock was ticking, and I had to decide soon. High school filled me with anxiety and the pressure to be perfect. I had to choose a lane and stay in it. After all, eighteen-year-olds should be able to know exactly what they want to do with the rest of their life, right?

Geez. What a ridiculous limiting belief.

My mother knew she wanted to be a lawyer when she was six years old, while I had six different career ideas a day. As the pressure mounted, and I looked around at all the "successful" people on paper in my life, I realized they had one thing in common—they were all miserable.

Yikes, I thought. *What am I in for?*

It can feel like there's no way out when you're in the thick of it. I remember when my world felt so small. All the heroes in my story were sad. *So,* I thought, *if this is how the heroes live, what's the point?* This led me to a very painful period of my life when I honestly thought trying to fit in wasn't worth it anymore. But despite the state of my mental health, proving a point to the people who said my family would never recover from their version of failure kept me going.

Instead of dealing with what was happening, I focused on excelling on paper instead. I had the grades to get into a great school, but first I had to choose one. I remember sitting with the guidance counselor as it became time to apply to universities.

"Well, what do you like?" he said.

I shrugged. "People. I just like connecting with people."

"Why don't you try public relations?"

So that's what I did, but not because I genuinely wanted to. I had to pick something or otherwise I'd be failing. I saw life as a linear series of events. After all, that's how success was marketed to us by the generations before. Get good grades, go to a good school, have a well-paying job, and fit in the well-constructed box of society.

How depressing.

I struggled internally with this box because I didn't believe I was meant for it. But I didn't know I could choose a different life either. What would people think if I failed?

I'd always wanted photography to be a part of my career, but I thought that it was as outrageous as being an actress. Of course, you can give it a try, but you should probably have a backup plan. So when I wasn't magically perfect at photography as a young teenager with no technical knowledge, I started leaning into my natural talents, which was understanding people, their needs, and how to market them.

With my new shiny piece of paper, I got my foot in the door to the marketing world. Did I love what I did? Some days. Very rarely. But I had an excellent salary, a stable job (or so I thought), and I could check things off the ultimate success checklist society had set out for me. Externally, I was killing it. Internally, it was killing me.

When Jim Carrey spoke about depression, I exhaled with understanding. It resonated with me deeply as I finally understood what had happened. He said depression is your body needing deep rest from the character you've been playing.

For years I'd played the character of a success-bound daughter who was independent, didn't need anyone, and could accomplish everything independently. Then, everything changed when the world shut down, and my warped version of success was ripped out from under me. How can you be successful when you have to give up your condo to move into your parents' basement, jobless, hopeless, and cut off from your extracurricular distractions? This shift really took a toll.

I was applying for jobs, but the competition was high and openings were slim, especially for someone who had just earned their diploma two years before the pandemic. I wallowed for a while. But then I decided to start creating my own versions of success with a different to-do list while handing out résumés like a mad woman.

I focused on my health.

I picked up a ridiculous number of hobbies.

I created my own "job," which included a schedule of meal prepping, working out, crafting, reading, learning Spanish, and anything that could be listed under the realm of self-improvement. I made sure that if there weren't any boxes I could tick off in my career, I was at least making banana bread and using Duolingo with the rest of society.

This mental stillness and break from the ever-addicting salary gave me clarity and a motivation for change. But it didn't give me enough confidence to start my own business. Instead, I took a job with a much lower salary in the small town of Collingwood, Ontario, two hours from my home.

I'd love to chalk it up to listening to my gut and taking a risk.

But the reality is, the Georgian Bay area was my retirement plan, and it was the first job offer that came my way. In looking back, I realize this was one of those moments when life wasn't happening to me, it was happening for me.

Default mode or dreams

Despite my whirlwind change in environment and people, I fell back into the same trusty default mode I always knew. I was going through the motions of what I thought was right while trying to figure out what I wanted. My dream was still photography, but I didn't think that was a career that would pay the bills. So I kept moving through the marketing industry with resentment. Yeah, I was good at it, but I hated my life from Monday to Friday and used the weekends to escape it rather than build a life I would be excited about.

I'd buy a lottery ticket here and there, hoping fate would intervene. And it did, in a sick, twisted way. My three-year-old cat suddenly became terribly ill. I barely took home $2,500 a month; she needed a $2,000 surgery. That's when I decided to try something outside the box. If I wasn't going to win the lottery, I would make shit happen myself.

I had the backbone of my incredibly strong mother to make things work despite the circumstances. And now was the time to discover what I really had in me. I knew I was good at a few things: I could write, manage social media, and create marketing plans. So I started figuring out how to sell those services online and through personal connections. I signed up for Upwork, an online freelancing community, and I worked evenings and weekends to start building my portfolio as a copywriter. While working online was easy money that didn't have a lot of overhead, I still felt a pull to pick up a camera, even though I had no idea how the heck to use one.

I was willing to work hard to build a business, but how I did it wasn't energetically sustainable. Long hours and little-to-no social life weren't ideal. I also wasn't following my dream but instead looking at the financial opportunities that were relatively low risk.

But then an opportunity came along. I was asked if I wanted to take before-and-after photos of a basement renovation for my stepdad. He worked with a property management company in the area. I thought, *Sure, why not?* I figure I would do it for free, and maybe I'd try it again if I was good at it. Looking back at those photos, I cringe. They aren't necessarily terrible, but they were not the quality I was expecting. I wanted no less than the perfection you see in *Our Homes* magazine. Because anytime you try something new, you should be perfect at it or stop trying, right? Ugh. Another terrible limiting belief I held close during that season of my life. It took me a ridiculous amount of time to capture that basement and edit the photos. Breaking that down, I was making about $12/hour.

I was surprised when they asked me to capture a condo because I didn't feel like my work was good enough. But that didn't stop me from trying. I was desperate to find as many income streams as I could to keep up with my cat's pricey food and my living expenses. I wanted photography to work more than anything, so I could actually love my job instead of just getting through the week. I knew I could get faster, so I committed myself to do the research instead of listening to the little voice that was terrified of failing.

I borrowed a realtor's camera, bought a second-hand lens, and paid someone I knew from my old marketing firm to teach me how to edit photos on Lightroom, a program I had never used before.

Simultaneously, I got a job offer from a company I had always dreamed of working with, plus an attractive salary and benefits package. Even though I had opportunities to go out on my own, my insecurity of failure won. I took the job and worked up to sixteen-hour days because I was too scared to fully believe in myself. Working nine to five in marketing and spending my evenings building my client base was a struggle. But a little voice in my head didn't want me to give up yet. Or maybe it was because of the bigger reason: I knew in my heart, this was meant to be.

After a month of this schedule and some severe burnout, I had to make a choice. I couldn't keep doing it all, and the pandemic taught me that a salary isn't guaranteed. So this time, I chose myself.

The decision to go entirely out of my comfort zone and give something a try catapulted my photography career. I began taking photos for this client regularly, who happened to onboard a ridiculous amount of Airbnbs that year. Word of mouth began to spread in the community about my photography, and I had enough copywriting clients to keep me busy with this beautiful balance.

It wasn't until I decided to be vulnerable and face rejection that everything changed for the better. It wasn't an easy journey. There is no automatic light switch to awesome. It takes daily habits, mindset shifts, and believing in yourself. Then one day, after some consistency, you wake up and realize you're finally living aligned with who you are, and you created your dream life.

Moving from living by default to living by design.

But I certainly wasn't done failing yet.

I had always wanted to try taking photos of people and step into the brand photo genre, but I was scared of doing a terrible job. The process between real estate photos and photos of people is wildly different. To top off the learning curve problem, I hate sucking at stuff. It's usually what prevents me from trying it or practicing. I said no for my first full year in business due to that limiting belief, even though deep down, I knew I wanted to. In a moment of courage, I asked my mom if I could practice on her.

It went terribly. I fumbled through it with awful lighting and then edited away on my PC. When the photos were as good as they were going to get, I sent them to my phone.

Um, what the heck? It looked like Trump's makeup artist had gotten ahold of her. She was so orange! After some research, I learned there's a significant color difference between PCs and Macs. They're not so big that I'd noticed in my previous twenty-five years of living, but they're big enough that skin tones are way off. Since most of us view things on an iPhone, I had to make a decision.

If I really wanted to try this, I had to commit and join the bo-ugee Mac family. So I invested, and that investment eventually came back tenfold. But I was still stuck due to limiting beliefs of failure and scared to chase the dream of capturing people. I wasn't ready to tell the world yet.

My next investment that changed my life happened by chance. I joined a coworking community with no expectations except for a place to land between photoshoots. I lived twenty-five minutes from most of my clients, so finding a space to edit between shoots so I didn't have to drive home was a plus.

But this wasn't just any ordinary coworking space. It was a community of like-minded people who would inspire me to operate as an authentic version of myself. They used Slack, an app, to connect its members through different channels. One of these channels would rotate biweekly and introduce you to someone and prompt a coffee date. That's how I met Paige.

I can't explain what it was, but there was an inner knowing that I had to work with her. I had never heard of neuro-linguistic programming (NLP), and the "woo-woo" world was considered a joke in the community I grew up in. NLP studies how our thoughts affect our behavior. Despite this stigma from my past, I decided to listen to that small voice and make an investment in myself.

Over the next three months, Paige shattered my limiting beliefs, and I healed from years of past trauma. It came to the surface that the choices I was making were to prove something to a community I was no longer a part of. I wasn't taking risks or believing in myself because I required external validation from people who didn't matter anymore and shouldn't have mattered in the first place. I was terrified of failure, and this was stalling my true calling and potential.

While I thought my past wasn't affecting my present, it was leaking into my life in more ways than I had cared to admit. Addressing this was the first step. After that realization, my inner voice became easier to hear. And I was finally ready to listen to her instead of numbing her.

I started saying yes to things before I felt ready to by trusting that I'd figure it out along the way. I made mistakes, but instead of letting them stop me, I allowed them to teach me. With each photo shoot, I got better. The world seemed to put the right people in my realm to help me reach my destiny.

Today, I still don't feel like I'm exactly where I want to be. But that isn't stopping me from trying new things, saying yes to opportunities that keep me curious, and learning along the way. I figured out that I might not even be aware of my true destination yet, so I may as well enjoy this journey. Oh yeah, and I ended up freelancing for *Our Homes* magazine as a photographer too. Everything truly came full circle.

When I started my photography career in real estate, it brought me to the beautiful world of branding. An overarching theme came to light when I sat down to think about why I loved it. Empowering people to amplify their awesomeness and express themselves authentically in this world is why I do what I do. And that led me to be curious about boudoir photography, which is the direction I'm currently heading. I still love capturing brands, but empowering women lights me up in a new way I want to explore.

You have the power

Your past doesn't define your destiny. You have the power to change the story. You ARE the main character, not a supporting role here to prove something. Your childhood is not your fault, but it is your responsibility to heal and become the person you know you're meant to be deep down. There is no winning lottery ticket that's going to save you from yourself. You have everything you need within. You just have to tap into it, ask for what you need, and say yes before you're ready. Get off default mode—your destiny is yours to design.

Life is unpredictable, and sometimes our plans don't work out as we hoped. But it's in those moments of dis-appointment and uncertainty that we have the chance to grow and discover new paths.

−AMANDA LEPIANE

NECESSITY IS THE MOTHER
OF ALL INVENTION.

To my husband, Peter.

AMANDA LEPIANE

Amanda LePiane is a social media manager, owner of Breeze Social Co., and mother of two based in Collingwood, Ontario. With her passion for creating communities and contributing to the growth of small businesses and social causes, Amanda has dedicated her career to changing the way we look at online marketing. Amanda's dedication to doing good wherever she goes is motivated by her desire to drive sales and business development for small business owners who want to make a positive difference in the world. Her authentic and kind approach has helped clients achieve their marketing goals.

@Breeze_Social
linkedin.com/in/amandalepiane

CHAPTER 4:
A CHANGE OF TUNE:
THE UNEXPECTED PATH
TO ENTREPRENEURSHIP

If you had asked the twelve-year-old me what I wanted to be when I grew up, I would have told you that I was going to be a musician. Not like a cool musician wearing leather pants and trashing hotel rooms, but the fancy-schmancy kind who played Mozart and Chopin.

Not many people currently in my life professionally know that I grew up playing in a marching band. Neat, right? Not only did I grow up playing in one, I literally spent most of every waking hour of my childhood studying music, rehearsing, and marching! Endless hours of rehearsing and practicing in rain, shine, or snow conditions. I am from Saskatchewan so snow was not out of the question.

It was an exciting time to be a nerd. I partook in numerous road trips to different parts of the United States to perform at large college football and NFL stadiums. I even marched in the Orange Bowl Parade when I was fifteen years old. I was fairly certain about what lay ahead of me after high school.

So off I went to study music education at the University of Regina, Saskatchewan. This particular course of study has you come out the other side as a music educator or a band or choir teacher to elementary or high school students. The pressure of university hit me like a ton of bricks. I was used to being a big fish in a small pond when I was in high school. I was used to being one of the more talented musicians and cleaned up in my last year when it came to music scholarships. Once in university, it took me a semester to get my shit together and really buckle down. High school hadn't really prepared me for the intensity of university life and study habits. I often think back to my home economics class where I learned to bake a cake and sew an apron. *Is this for real?* I wondered as a fifteen-year-old. And where were the male students when I was baking and sewing? When tax time rolls around each spring, I often think of that bloody apron and wonder why we weren't taught bookkeeping in high school "economics."

After three years studying classical music at university, I was told by my doctor I had carpal tunnel syndrome. I was so shocked by this diagnosis. Wasn't that something that older people got? In hindsight, I shouldn't have been surprised. My hand and arm constantly ached after hours and hours of practicing my flute each day. My hand had become somewhat useless to me since I couldn't carry things or open doors without feeling uncomfortable. It was bothersome to write notes at school too. Yes, I went to university before there were computers in classrooms, so notes were taken by hand, not on a laptop or iPad.

At the end of my third year, I decided to face my reality, get wrist surgery to alleviate some of the discomfort, and move to Vancouver to study fashion merchandising. It was a total 180-degree turn from my previous career path, I know! The whole heartbreaking end to my music career path left me wondering where I went from there. And where I was, was a constant reminder of a dream that was lost.

Embracing change and finding new paths

It was difficult to accept that the thing I had dedicated so much time and effort to was no longer a viable career option for me. The idea of starting over and completely changing course was daunting. But I knew I couldn't let the disappointment and frustration of my failed dream hold me back from pursuing other opportunities.

The recovery from surgery was slow and super painful. But during that time, I had a chance to reflect on my future and what I really wanted to do with my life. I had always loved fashion and had a keen eye for trends and styling. I realized that pursuing a career in fashion merchandising could be a fulfilling and exciting option for me.

I threw myself into my studies, soaking up every bit of knowledge I could about the fashion industry. I took on internships and worked hard to build my skills and experience. It wasn't easy, but I was determined to make the most of my new path and not let fear or doubt hold me back.

Looking back now, I see how my setback was actually a blessing in disguise. It forced me to step out of my comfort zone, take risks, and explore new opportunities. It was a painful lesson, but it taught me the importance of resilience, adaptability, and the value of pursuing multiple passions.

Man, life is unpredictable, and sometimes our plans don't work out as we hoped. But it's in those moments of disappointment and uncertainty that we have the chance to grow and discover new paths. I remind myself of this *all the time*. It's important to embrace change and to keep moving forward, even if it means starting over. You never know where life will take you, and sometimes the unexpected turns can lead to the most rewarding experiences.

Fashion school was as fun as you're probably imagining: funky-dressed young people tearing through the latest *Vogue*. Huddling together to cram for exams. Memorizing which designer designs for which house, as well as naming all of their signature design looks, their muses, and what they were known for. We learned how to do retail math, sketch, and style outfits. I crushed it at the retail math course, hence my later career choice as a fashion buyer.

Cut to twenty years later and a few career moves and I am now the founder and owner of a small social media agency in beautiful Collingwood, Ontario, called Breeze Social Co. In all honesty, owning and operating my very own "small but mighty" (as I like to say) business was not something I even really considered or aspired to for up until five years ago.

Taking a leap: learning to go slow and steady in entrepreneurship

How did this happen? Well, at the beginning of the COVID pandemic, much like many other Torontonians, my husband, kids, and I fled the city as soon as we could sell our house. Having dreamed of and planned on retiring away from the ding ding of Toronto's bustle, my husband and I wondered if we could steal a little bit of retirement time while our kids were small, while we could make bold moves, and most importantly, while I had the courage to take a leap of faith and start my own business.

It's said that necessity is the motherhood of all invention, and boy is that right! Since I've always loved social media (rare, I know), my husband actually recommended I start my own consultancy to work in it, which I thought was nuts. I'd always been so comfortable having a "job" and workin' it to get that 2 percent raise each year. Being a fashion buyer has some *major* perks. Exciting travel to places like Hong Kong and New York, free swag, and countless cool experiences and five-star meals. How in the world would I steer my own ship, sell my business offerings, and manage my own books and cash flow?

Like any almost forty-year-old, I surveyed all my besties about this plan. To my surprise, I was told to go for it! Really? By all of them? Yes, by all of them. One friend in particular, Lesley, who runs several successful businesses of her own, offered the most valuable piece of advice: go slow. At first I wasn't quite sure what she meant, but her words have stayed with me over the years. Whenever I feel tempted to rush into something, I remind myself to take a breath and consider my options carefully. I've learned that taking the time to grow and adapt to change is essential for long-term success in any field, especially in the fast-paced world of social media. Lesley's wisdom has saved me from burnout and helped me approach my work with a more measured and strategic mindset.

Going back to school was a rude awakening. I remember feeling the perfect storm of excitement, overwhelm, and im-postor syndrome setting in on day one. I was by far the oldest in our class. Cringe. I had to remind myself why I was doing this. There was no turning back now. So, we took the plunge and moved away from Toronto, and suddenly there were no corporate jobs to head back to without subjecting myself to hours of commuting. The thought of having to leave those adorable roundabouts nestled among the green lake and mountains in the backdrop lit a fire under my butt. I was definitely going to figure this out—I HAD to figure this out.

In the end, I made it through a digital marketing course at Brain Station and managed not to get "okay boomered" by the cool twenty-somethings. I absolutely learned a lot, but most importantly, I learned that there are many things in digital marketing I don't want to do. Funny, right? I remember telling my husband that maybe I'd wasted time and money on this course. His reply was "Uh, no, you invested money to find out what you don't want to do. Now go after what lights you up." I see that now. Investing in myself is never a waste of money.

In my adorable community of Collingwood, we have a rather large and ferociously connected entrepreneurial circle that I immediately joined. The vibe is always collaboration over competition, and "netgiving" over networking. One of the first events I attended was led by a guest speaker who spoke about finding your ideal client and focusing on that to help grow and streamline your business. That lovely guest speaker was Amanda Wilson-Ciocci. She is my business coach and continues to help shape my business and give me perspective when I am lost in the woods. Investing in a business coach was another great decision I made because my husband told me to go for it! That's the thing about entrepreneurship: you are doing it alone but alone with many other people going it alone, too.

As a working mother, I had always struggled to balance my career and my family. The long hours and brutal commute left me feeling exhausted and disconnected from my kids. So after much consideration, I decided to take some time off to be a stay-at-home mom. At first, it was a difficult transition. I missed the structure of my job and the social interactions with my colleagues.

But as time went on, I began to relish the opportunity to focus solely on my children and our home. I spent my days preparing endless bite-sized meals, exploring new parks and playgrounds, and hosting playdates with other stay-at-home parents and their little ones.

It wasn't always easy, of course. There were tantrums and messes and moments of frustration. But in the midst of it all, I knew I was creating memories that would last a lifetime. My kids were thriving, and I felt a sense of purpose and fulfillment that I had never experienced before. Looking back on that time, I realize how lucky I was to have had the opportunity to be a stay-at-home mom. Now that my kids are older and more independent, I'm grateful for the special bond we created during those years.

I realize this next part is a tale as old as time. Most corporate-world workers who join the entrepreneurial space have horror stories about their corporate experience including too many long hours that go unrecognized and not enough money.

But my decision to leave corporate life behind and start my own business wasn't just about escaping the long hours and shitty commute. Don't get me wrong, those were definitely factors. The real reason, however, was that I needed to go it alone and see what stuff I was really made of. I wanted to take ownership of my work and create something that truly reflected my values and goals. The corporate world had taught me a lot, but it didn't give me the creative freedom or the sense of purpose I craved.

I truly used to believe that once one finished school, they got a job and that was their career path. Sure, they may bounce from company to company, but they are on a path until retirement. The world certainly doesn't have to work that way anymore. Today, I spend my days working as a freelance social media manager helping various clients create and curate content for their online presence.

My work involves managing social media accounts, creating engaging posts, responding to comments and messages, and analyzing performance metrics. Apart from that, I also spend time networking with potential clients and keeping up with the latest trends and best practices in the social media industry. Working for different clients and industries keeps me challenged and allows me to continuously learn and improve my skills. While my career path may not be traditional, I love the flexibility and freedom it provides me, and I feel fulfilled knowing that I am making a positive impact on the businesses I work with.

I hope I've reminded you of the importance of resilience and adaptability in achieving your dreams. Although I faced the challenge of carpal tunnel syndrome and had to change my career path, I didn't give up on my aspirations. Instead, I embraced my new direction and built my skills and experience in a different field, eventually founding my own social media agency. So, remember to pursue multiple passions, stay open to unexpected opportunities, and take it slow.

Do the thing that scares you and lights you up.
Do the thing that both your seven-year-old self
and future self would be proud of.

-JODIE HEFFREN

AS I STARTED MAKING DECISIONS THAT
SCARE ME AND PULL ME OUT OF MY
COMFORT ZONE, I REALIZED THAT THIS IS
WHERE BIG CHANGE COMES FROM. AND
IT'S IN THE DISCOMFORT WHERE DREAMS
COME TO FRUITION.

To my daughters: you are the reason I had the courage to go down
this path in the first place. May you always walk your truth, for
within it you find the greatest gifts. To my husband, Kyle: thank you
for your unwavering support and for every sacrifice that stretches
the boundaries of your to-do list. To Rachel, my ride or die, and
to Kathryn, my Inner Child Healing Coach: thank you for opening
my world to the opportunity to heal, get uncomfortable, and grow.
And to my family, friends (especially my Wild Sisters), and those
who have guided, mentored, and supported me: I am fortunate to
say there are too many of you to name. Thank you for holding me
accountable and loving me unconditionally.

JODIE HEFFREN

Jodie Heffren, a registered nurse, courageously pursued her dream of embracing life to the fullest. Escaping the hustle and bustle of city life, she found solace and inspiration in the serene embrace of nature. As a reflector in human design, she now shares her gift of healing and tranquility through Rooted Woodland experiences, her sanctuary for nurturing self-discovery and well-being that invites you to embrace life to the fullest with courage and love. Jodie resides with her loving husband and two cherished daughters on 42 acres, where she illuminates the path of self-discovery for all who cross her path.

@ROOTEDWOODLAND

WWW.ROOTEDWOODLAND.COM

CHAPTER 5:
TRUTH BUMPS

The phrase "dark night of the soul" is described in the *Psychiatric Times* as an extremely difficult period in one's life, such as the death of a loved one, the breakup of a marriage, or any other moment of heartbreak. Going through extreme difficulty is a time of pain, but it also presents an opportunity for personal development, self-discovery, and profound change.

My reason for sharing my journey is to give hope, inspiration, and a little nudge to you if you feel like you need it to take that first/next step toward creating the life you desire. You really are just one decision away from changing the trajectory of your life. No one accomplishes new things or crushes their goals from within their comfort zone—it's in the discomfort where the magic happens, and consciously deciding to embrace dis-comfort is an act of courage. I am proof of this and will share that here with you. Repeat after me: "I am courageous. I am brave. I can do hard things." Notice how you feel and write this affirmation on your mirror or in your journal where you can frequently see it. If you say it enough, you will start to believe it, if you don't already.

Honor your season

I believe it's important to honor the time and season of your life that you are in. We are all in different seasons and you need to do what works for you wherever you are. Enjoy the season, and when you are ready, break down the barriers holding you back from the life you desire.

My inspiration to share my story is my two daughters. What I have come to realize is that by showing up as someone who is learning and growing into the best version of myself, and allowing my kids to witness that, allows them to grow up knowing that it is okay—that it's encouraged—that they show up for themselves first and know that the goal is always progress, never perfection.

Despite what my parents say, there is nothing inherently different about me, so my story is relatable. I grew up in the suburbs of a small town in southwestern Ontario, Canada, in the eighties. My father worked as a public servant and my mother was a figure-skating coach turned real estate agent. I was a regular kid with a little brother whose parents split when I was seven. I was brought up with rules and encouraged to strive for nothing less than perfection. I wasn't allowed to take a year off after high school, despite not having a clue what I wanted to do for the rest of my life. I wasn't a rebel, something that may be my only regret. I am fortunate that I am still best friends with the person I met in grade three. Maybe you can relate to parts of my story. Honestly, "if I can do it, you can do it" is such a cliché, but I can't find the words to say it any fancier or simpler than that. There is no reason that you can't do the things that you want to do. I recognize that I am writing this as a privileged white woman who has a supportive husband, that we are in good health and have jobs that pay our bills. So, this is the perspective where I am writing from today and recognize that not everyone has the same.

When I called my parents and told them I said yes to coauthor a book, they both said that they were proud of me and neither sounded surprised. I think I was more surprised that I was coauthoring a book than either of them. My mother's next words were: "How are you doing this? How are you constantly taking action these days? You were not always like this; I see that there has been a big shift."

The new thing I started doing is literally *doing the thing*. I have no idea HOW I am doing it, but I am not worrying about how. As Adele Tevlin often says on her podcast, the *how* is none of my business. I understood that being offered the opportunity to write a chapter in this book was an incredible opportunity that gave me full-body goosebumps (what I refer to as "truth bumps"), and it scared the shit out of me. I knew it was an opportunity that is connected to my *why*. And it was a "HELL YES" not a "Ho-hum, yeah, I guess." It was a barf-bag moment. It literally made me feel sick to my stomach when I replied to Amanda by saying "I'm in!" But I knew I had to do it precisely because it scared me and filled me with nervous excitement.

As I started making decisions that scare me and pull me out of my comfort zone, I realized that this is where big change comes from. And it's in the discomfort where dreams come to fruition. I am doing it scared, doing it vulnerable, doing it full of uncertainty, and doing it with my whole heart.

As I think back to myself in 2018, that version of me would be shocked to hear where I am now, just five years from the time she said yes to herself. That version of me would have thought, *Sure sounds nice for someone else, but that will never happen to me.* The 2018 version of me was lost and tired, and she had a lack of motivation in the depths of motherhood. With a three-year-old and one-year-old in tow, I was working full-time shift work, managing household duties, and showing up for everyone except myself. That wasn't new, though, as it was how I'd lived most of my life: doing the things I should do and was expected to do (both by myself and others). I never gave any thought to changing the pattern I knew. That version of me had no idea what she wanted to be when she grew up. I said that for a lot of my adult life, even a decade into my nursing career. I often felt lost and as though I wasn't living for myself. I wasn't living the life I desired—I felt really stuck. Don't get me wrong, I loved the life my husband and I were creating. I loved him and being a mother to our daughters, but my desire for a fulfilling life ran deeper than that. I felt like I was coasting, maybe even taking the easy route. I came to realize I no longer wanted to live on the surface of my life; I wanted to dive in deep.

What I didn't realize then but have learned on this journey is that I was never lost. I was always there, hiding under the expectations I put on myself and the expectations that society put on me. The overall conditioning I grew up to know led me to believe that I couldn't listen to the little twinges (my intuition) that tried to guide me to the answers—the conditioning that shushed the dreams of being creative and loudly proclaimed the practical things. It was only through the process of unschooling and unlearning many of the things that the world forced onto me that I have been able to see more clearly, with my own eyes, the life that brings me fulfillment, satisfaction, and joy. I was very comfortable in my life. But I was uncomfortable with who I was within my life. It never occurred to me to do anything that made me uncomfortable. Why would I voluntarily step out of my comfort zone? But I realized that I would never see the change in my life that I longed for as long as I stayed comfortable. It wasn't a lightbulb moment but more of a glimpse into my future while listening to a colleague talk about their life. She was talking about not rocking the boat of change in order to keep things calm in her household. It was like she was holding up a mirror and I saw myself in her actions. That's when I realized I wasn't living for my own life. I acknowledged that discomfort in my body and decided I needed to take action. My story is one of how one decision to step out of my comfort zone started a journey of working with a coach to work through generational trauma that transformed into me finding the truest version of myself. Taking the first step into discomfort is the start of actually feeling comfortable within.

The interesting thing is that for as long as I can remember, when people have asked, "If you won the lottery and didn't need to work, what would you do with your time?" I had the same answer: "I would be a party planner, but only for people who I align with, and it will be in nature. They will be events that I can wholeheartedly get behind." When I finally listened, really listened, to my inner voice about what I wanted to do with my life, I started to make it happen. I decided to transition from nursing to nature and begin living the life I had been dreaming about. And that's precisely what I'm now doing with my business, Rooted Woodland. One of my goals is to help people come back to nature where things are quiet so they can find the direction they want to go in. I now plan and host intimate events and retreats for people to find themselves in nature. I have done my certification to guide others through the transformation of breathwork and deliberate cold exposure. I am doing all that I can to help others step into discomfort to help them find the truest version of themselves. At Rooted Woodland, "Nature is not just a place you visit, it is where you find yourself."

This first step included saying yes to me by making myself a priority. I realized that I had to take care of myself so I could show up as a better, truer version of me. The first decision I made was to join a women's group where I was surrounded with other like-minded women who had a similar goal of self-rediscovery. They taught me the power of vulnerability and the amazing things that can happen when you share what is really going on in your life (the real shit, not the stuff you talk about on the subway). I will be forever grateful to that group of women, many of whom are still actively in my life today. And as scary as it was, when it was my turn to share, I never felt judged, which is remarkable because I've felt judged my entire life. From my family and friends to complete strangers, I've never felt allowed (in my mind) to be my whole authentic self. But these women gave me permission (that I thought I needed) to open up a part of me that I've always kept hidden. The permission came when I witnessed others' bravery and courage as they put themselves out there, raw and vulnerable, and shared their pain. One woman shared about her struggles with her mother-wound and the clarity and growth she developed from working with an Inner Child Healing Coach. I had no idea such a coach existed. I had recently come to recognize the feeling of my intuition (the little twinges) so went on to have my free consultation call with her coach, and wow! I got more out of that consultation than I did with any previous therapist. I can say with one-hundred-percent certainty that working with my Inner Child Healing Coach transformed my life, as she gave me the tools to tap into the highest version of my authentic self. I have come to recognize that vulnerability is a superpower. It has been through embracing my vulnerability that the door has opened to my own personal growth, creating authentic connections, emotional resilience, and self-acceptance. It is here where I have unlocked my true potential and created a more fulfilling and meaningful life.

I have been fostering a judgment-free community and encouraging vulnerability since I launched the first retreat at Rooted Woodland in January 2023. Around the opening circle I share parts of my story in hopes of helping others and encouraging the magic that comes from within when you feel safe and encouraged to share. As Brené Brown says, "Vulnerability is not winning or losing; it's having the courage to show up and be seen when we have no control over the outcome. Vulnerability is not weakness; it's our greatest measure of courage."

I am not that far down the path from the person reading this who wants to make a change and wants to go for it, but she might just need a little nudge. Let this be it. I followed my intuition (after learning how to listen to it) and started saying yes to the things that scared me but also excited me. I didn't know how I was going to pay for the business coaching I wanted and felt I needed. I convinced myself to not worry about the *how* because on this journey I have learned that the *how* is not up to us. If it's meant to happen, it will when it is meant to.

I am just beginning, and I still have bouts of major impostor syndrome, especially being among this group of inspiring writers; however, I recognize that each of us who are collaborating on this book have been where you are. We have all experienced the barf-bag moments of saying yes to something that scares us—of launching an event or a product without actually feeling ready for the day to come. We have all said yes to the scary thing that gives us the full-body truth bumps because we know it is the way to our higher selves. It has taken each of us down a similar path, yet we all hold very different stories and experiences that led us to where we are today.

Facing fears

I love biking, but I developed a fear of cycling anywhere but on a nice smooth trail. Maybe it happened after working as an ER nurse where I saw my fair share of traumas, or maybe it's because I am a forty-year-old woman who doesn't bounce like I once did. When we moved to a place where mountain biking is a way of life, I decided to face my fear. Repeating Glennon

Doyle's words to myself, "I can do hard things!" I signed up for a women's beginner mountain biking course. And this will be my mantra as I climb and descend the hills, go over the rocks and under the branches. When I saw it advertised, it was another "Hell yes!" for me, so I signed up before it was too late. We are now three weeks in, and I am having so much fun. I am learning to let go of control and trust my bike (a true metaphor for life's journey). When I sit on my bike, I really tap into my inner child, and she would be really proud of me today.

Joining a women's group, following my intuition to move two and a half hours from our life, going from downtown living to 42 acres of forest where we don't know anyone, then starting a business with no background in entrepreneurship are just a few of the things that I have recently done that scared me. They're all out of my comfort zone, yet they are all things that have taken me from the surface of my life to the depths where I feel fulfilled.

What do you have an interest in doing but you have felt too scared to say yes to? I challenge you to trust in those truth bumps, face your fear, and say yes.

So, I really did know what I wanted to be when I grew up, I just kept pushing that version of myself down and didn't let her develop. I didn't even give her a damn chance! Surround yourself with women who inspire you, who you learn from, and who let you show up unapologetically. The people who support, encourage, and challenge you and hold you account-able—those are who you want in your circle. If it wasn't for the badass women I have within reach, I wouldn't have survived the writing process for this chapter or had the confidence to continue a few months into launching Rooted Woodland. So let this be a lesson that you can do hard things too! Say yes to the things that light you up, that give you truth bumps, and that make you think "HELL YES!" Say no to the rest. Audition for the theater production, register for guitar lessons, sign up for a house exchange. Do the thing that scares you and lights you up. Do the thing that both your seven-year-old self and future self would be proud of. After all, you are only one decision away from living the life of your dreams, and no one can make that happen but you.

Your dark night of the soul may bring about intense feelings of pain and many challenges, but it can be a necessary stage for personal and spiritual growth. It presents as an opportunity for introspection, healing, and letting go of old patterns and beliefs that no longer align with you. You'll come out on the other side of it with a revitalized understanding of yourself with clarity and a deeper spiritual connection. As I continue within the new journey of entrepreneurship from the "getting started" phase into the "getting in a groove" phase, I can't help but get really excited about what's to come next. One thing I know for sure: when I get those full-body truth bumps about that next thing, I will be saying yes and pushing through the discomfort. I look forward to seeing you on the other side.

We've imagined this world into being with our fears, so why can't we imagine another more beautiful one into being with our love?

−NONA MORROW

IF IT FEELS LIKE YOUR LIFE IS ON A DOWN-SWING AND THINGS AREN'T WORKING OUT AS PLANNED, MY HEART GOES OUT TO YOU. I'D LIKE YOU TO KNOW THAT NO MATTER WHAT YOU'VE ENDURED, WHAT YOU THINK OR HAVE BEEN TOLD, YOU HAVE THE POTENTIAL POWER IN YOU TO TRANSFORM YOUR ENTIRE EXPERIENCE OF LIFE IN WAYS YOU MAY HAVE NEVER IMAGINED.

To Scott, my best friend and husband of more than thirty years. Your unconditional love has been the greatest gift in my life. To my boys, Gord and Charlie, thank you for teaching me how to give that love, and to my parents and beloved extended family for all of your support. Last but not least, to the higher self in all of us: may we remember who we truly are and allow ourselves to rise above and beyond the shackles of lack, limitation, ignorance, and fearful thinking of this world to the freedom, well-being, and peace that lay beyond.

REV NONA MORROW

Rev Nona Morrow is a minister, a member of The Canadian International Metaphysical Ministry, and has been a Life Coach for over twenty-five years. She was mentored by Marianne Williamson and certified as a "Miracle-Minded Coach." Her work is focused on helping others find a deep sense of inner peace, fulfillment, and freedom by shifting from fear to love. Nona is the author of "The Field" and creator of "The Shift." She and her husband, Scott, have two grown boys. They live in Collingwood, Ontario, with their golden retriever, Gracie.

NONAMORROW.SUBSTACK.COM
@NONAMORROW

CHAPTER 6:
OUR NATURE

I had to pee . . . BADLY. But it was 1 o'clock in the morning and I could hear something rustling in the bushes outside of my tent. I was in the middle of Africa by myself, far from everything familiar, with only a nylon tent between me and the unidentified heavy breathing rummager outside. Earlier that day I had seen hippos sunbathing lazily in the river. They didn't seem threatening until I heard someone say that hippos kill more tourists every year in Africa than any other animal. I took a deep breath and exhaled slowly, trying to coax myself to relax and not overreact. My mind jumped to the side effects of Mefloquine, the anti-malarial drug that I had taken for my trip, which has since been taken off the market: "May cause paranoia." I needed to get a grip.

Now I REALLY had to go.

I made the bold decision to just stick my bum outside of my tent but stay hidden under the "fly." Instant relief. I slowly and stealthily zipped myself back into my tent and stayed as still as possible while holding my breath and hoping that the mystery wildling would wander off.

It didn't.

I watched wide-eyed as the top of my tent started to luff and buckle under an outside force.

My mind went blank. I shivered as I imagined how a giant incisor piercing my vital organs would feel and how long it would take me to bleed out. My whole body began to shake, and then I prayed. That's the last thing I remember from that night.

When I opened my eyes, it hit me as I quickly scrambled to sit up in my sleeping bag . . . I'M ALIVE! I sensed the early morning pre-dawn dewy stillness. I realized that I must have either passed out from exhaustion or fainted in fear. As I carefully unzipped my tent to climb out, the first thing I noticed was that I had peed RIGHT in my Birkenstocks. Doh. I scrambled out and I smelled it before I saw it: my hand covered my mouth as it dropped open with the realization that an elephant had taken a massive SH*T on my tent.

The mental image of a big gray bum lined up on top of me made me laugh out loud. Life had LITERALLY JUST taken a GIANT steamer on me. I gratefully sat and sipped my coffee and watched the sun rise over the river feeling somehow different than I did the day before. I felt alive.

Then something unexpected happened . . .

From out of nowhere hundreds of dung beetles came marching toward me in unison. Like a purposeful parade, they boldly veered toward my tent. They mobilized quickly and made ping-pong–sized balls of poop and rolled them backward with their hind legs in what can best be described as synchronized perfection. It was one of the most incredible things I've ever witnessed.

The entire poop evac was completed in under two hours, and I later learned that it would soon become a cozy breeding chamber and fuel to feed this army of holy rollers who would use the Milky Way to navigate back to their tunnels.

Sometimes in fleeting moments, like when I'm watching a sunrise or sunset or when a deer crosses my path, I feel a deep sense of awe and reverence at the sheer diversity of life on this planet. Buddhist monk Thích Nhat Hahn had a name that describes us perfectly: "Interbeings." The perfection of our whole ecosystem and all the little things we take for granted that make our lives possible are so mind-boggling when you really stop and think about them. Just the fact that what we breathe out, the trees breathe in, and what the trees breathe out, we breathe in fills me with wonder.

My trip to Africa was in the early 1990s when I was in my early twenties and really had no idea what life had in store for me. I've had my fair share of highs and lows—times when nothing seemed to go wrong, and others when it felt like life WAS taking a massive crapper on me. While the details of our personal stories may vary, I suspect that despite the differences in our narratives, it was the hard times that shaped our character and molded our hearts to have more empathy for others and to help us realize that we have the capaciousness to hold it all and keep moving forward one day at a time.

If it feels like your life is on a downswing and things aren't working out as planned, my heart goes out to you. I'd like you to know that no matter what you've endured, what you think or have been told, you have the potential power in you to transform your entire experience of life in ways you may have never imagined. Saints and sages have been pointing to this possibility since the beginning of time, but it has mostly flown under our cultural radar with our predominantly materialist worldview. But more and more of us are experiencing a massive shift in consciousness. Quantum physics, leading-edge psychology, noetic science, and the study of consciousness are thriving areas of research in neuroscience, and best of all, they align perfectly with ancient non-dual teachings.

This is exactly what famous psychologist Abraham Maslow realized before his death in 1970. He confessed after his own personal awakening that his own "hierarchy of needs" that was published in the mid-1950s was incomplete. Even though we are still teaching his original pyramid, he realized that the old peak experience of "self-actualization" as it was described is NOT the peak or final step, "transcendence" is. A person is motivated not only by realizing personal potential and self-ful-fillment and seeking personal growth and peak experiences but ultimately by values that transcend beyond the personal self, which is what spiritual teachers like Jesus and Buddha have been pointing to. We have just missed it; it's been RIGHT under our noses ALL along.

Powerful inner shifts

There are so many real-life examples of people who have ex-perienced this subtle but powerful inner shift and have freed themselves from their limiting beliefs, anxiety, and deep depres-sions. Some have had a near-death experience or defied the odds by experiencing an inexplicable, spontaneous remission from an advanced inoperable stage of a disease that shifted their worldview, and many spend the rest of their lives feeling compelled to better understand their experience.

There is something about the nature of our suffering that makes us more humble and present, which leads us to see something in the natural world we couldn't seem to access before to transcend our ego and have the instant and complete mouth-dropping realization that we are not our suffering or the shit that happens to us but a powerful creative part of this whole beautiful dance of life. In that sense, my elephant story is analogous for all of us.

It seems like the natural world provides all the metaphors that the soul needs for its growth, and I can see now that our life challenges are a brilliant tailor-made curriculum to help us grow into the fullness of who we really are.

We can even use our challenges to experience something new that may never have been possible.

Do you know where male peacocks get their beautiful colors? By eating poisonous thorns. It's built IN for us to learn about our nature with all of creation. When we are disconnected from our true power we feel like we need to take matters into our own hands and get busy defending, planning, improving, controlling, fixing, medicating, numbing, or managing in a feeble attempt to affect changes at the level of effect to prevent future suffer-ing, which gives us the false illusion that we're protected and in control. When the turds inevitably DO fall, our task masters start beavering away before nature can even take its course.

Alternatively, we may convince ourselves there is something wrong with us and we need to look outside of ourselves for help. We forget that the nature of the universe is self-organizing and self-correcting and tends to run better without our interference the same way the atmosphere did when we shut down operations during COVID. The air became visibly clearer almost overnight once nature had an opportunity to do her thing unimpeded by us. The same is true for the nature of our inner experience and how we see ourselves in the world and relate to one another.

There is a highly intelligent primary organizing principle at play inside of ourselves and by simply aligning to it and being inwardly guided we can follow the cosmic crumbs and find a better way.

That's what life is asking of us: to see and experience this for ourselves.

It's good news. We can stop running out to buy shovels and wheelbarrows or do anything with our sh*t; it will be cleared away. We've all heard the saying "Let go and let God." It's like a message for all of us to RELAX. When we align to the power greater than us, we will be guided if there is action that needs taking—and then we're good to go, but not a moment before and never from our own best thinking and solo efforts.

When we brace for the worst and live in fear and anxiety, we unwittingly create chaos, stress, and illness, and we even unconsciously block our dreams from manifesting with every fearful lack-filled thought that crosses our minds. I know because that was my modus operandi and I was VERY good at it! We even have the power to deplete our own resources, crash our stock markets, and disrupt the supply of toilet paper when we panic.

Spending years of our lives examining the content or the narrative about the poop is also not going to change anything at the level of cause. It may make us feel better at the time to hash things up and feel heard, but ultimately it's not a great way to spend our lives dwelling on the past. Knowing where it came from and what's in the poop doesn't ever make it go away. In fact, since we're divine creators with our sustained and focused energy and attention on it, we are assured a LOT more dung in the days ahead.

There's a spiritual principle from the teachings in "A Course in Miracles" that a "miracle" is a shift in perception. When we change how we see something, that something changes. The metaphysical and spiritual texts I have read over the years have begun to make literal sense. They are not just intellectual or theological concepts to me anymore. They are all pointing DI-RECTLY to this. At the time, I wasn't sure how long any of it would last, but I was astounded that this state was even potential in me. I still am. In the same way I remember being surprised by contractions when I was pregnant with my firstborn. As giant muscular spasms ripped through me, I thought, *Wow, I've had this body for three decades, and I never really knew my body could do this!* (Just like that, but more fun!)

Looking back, I can trace it back to an ending: struggling with a decade-long depression that I tried to hide from others behind my optimism and warm smile, topped off with debilitating chronic pain, which eventually resulted in two hip replacements, cyclical weight gain and loss, and an inability to walk or move freely. I felt like I was stuck in my story and a victim of my circumstances. I wanted so badly to free myself, and it was like I was standing in quicksand: the harder I struggled to get out, the deeper I sank.

I felt a deep longing that I couldn't seem to fill. I had a deep sense that there was more to life than this suffering. In one vulnerable moment shortly after asking for help and literally falling to my knees and praying to better understand my own true nature, I was invited to see a simple but light-filled beautiful Universal truth . . .

THERE IS NOTHING WRONG WITH ME!

I had instant and immediate access to a new depth of understanding that everything I experienced was coming from my own conscious awareness and thoughts. This was a TOTAL game changer.

I can clearly remember covering my mouth with my hand in disbelief. In a moment of clarity, ALL my previously perceived problems fell away in one fell swoop along with my fears, anxiety, addictive tendencies, and any remnants of doubt with this recognition of my true nature. It was like they were being carried away on their own accord or rolled away by some angelic army of invisible dung beetles.

I can remember laughing at how ridiculous and inconvenient this insight was because we've built an entire empire and economy around our fearful imaginings. It felt like waking up from a dream. I felt this incredulous sense wondering HOW had I not seen or experienced this before?

It also occurred to me that it was so simple that no one would even believe it, or me.

Soon after it dawned on me that all the stuff that has happened in my life has been a kind of fertilizer for me to grow and evolve to see this for myself. It took me five decades and who knows how many lifetimes to crack myself open, but all along with the struggling, some part of me KNEW that there was more to me all along. More to you. I just KNEW IT!

It's time for us to shift away from fear and reconnect to life. Reconnect to our essence and learn from the natural world. Reconnect to what's deepest in us.

Raising our Spiritual Quotient and awareness IS the key and has been all along.

Religion and yoga can help bind us back into our true selves, but the practices we do or the faith we grew up with may not even be beautiful or intelligent enough to answer our big questions. We may need to deconstruct our inherited concepts of God to connect directly with the source of our being to have an experience of this for ourselves. I can clearly see now that there is no such thing as THE way, but ALL spiritual traditions are pointing us to this potent power and light within us.

I am 100 percent certain that you are enough as you are.

I don't expect you to believe me. You can't because it's impossible for our egos to swallow this whole. On top of that, admitting we don't know something doesn't come easily to us. We want to see it before we believe it, but our senses can deceive us. Like those dung beetles, we tend to focus on our day-to-day experience, just making the best of the crap that's right in front of us.

I've had an incredible life and I've seen and experienced so many wonderful moments, but this realization is by far THE best thing that has ever happened to me. It has rendered EV-ERYTHING sublime, even the shitty bits. ALL of it feels divine to me now.

I trust life and the loving and abundant still-small voice INSIDE of me now, not what the world projects at me in fear and lack. If I'm being honest, becoming a minister and sticking my neck out on social media to talk about our concepts of God, love, and ego transcendence was not something I'd have EVER imagined as a desirable career path. It's counter cultural on a good day and certainly not being done for the money, although ironically, along with this understanding comes the innate power to man-ifest whatever is needed to serve, something I could never quite grasp when I lived in fear, doubt, and lack.

This experience was enough to change my whole worldview and the trajectory of my life. All I want to do now is to find creative, fun, and inclusive ways to help others interested in experiencing this inner shift for themselves. The practicality of these spiritual teachings is so far beyond our human understanding that it's no wonder we reject them and our concepts of God or Source or even live in the denial of the Divine for our own good reasons, but this is not a religious thing. It's a human thing. We're not the separate beings we've convinced ourselves that we are.

Aligning with love

We've imagined and manifested our lives and this world into being with our fears, so why can't we imagine another more beautiful one aligned with nature into being with our love?

It's our disconnection from our true nature that is at the root of all human cruelty and environmental degradation, and it's our connection that can heal the world. It feels to me like we are not here learning how to be love, we ARE love learning how to be here.

As a high school history and geography teacher, I observed the sobering truth long ago staring right back at me from every history book that after thousands of years we are simply not learning from our mistakes. Even with the beautiful ecumenical truths and scientific discoveries right at our fingertips, it's clear that humanity will not wake up on its own—the ego devices in our minds have been so tightly secured like a horse blinder that our vision is blocked to see this for ourselves, and we've taken a giant detour into fear with our powerfully creative minds.

The GOOD news is that you are only ONE decision away from the biggest transformation of your entire life, and it's like nothing you could ever imagine.

If you're interested to learn more about this understanding, I write weekly inspirational essays and notes in "The Field." You never know when the next elephant's derriere will be teetering overhead, but now you know that there is nothing to fear. A bit of fertilizer in the form of a life challenge can go a long way to help us recognize our own true nature from the seed of love that was in us all along.

The answers you are seeking are closer than you could ever imagine.

This understanding is not difficult, but it is different. It's not something to strive for, but it's innate in you. If you're ready to experience a shift in your life, simply become willing and open-minded to the possibility. You will be naturally guided to take the next necessary steps to find your way, just like the dung beetles used the Milky Way to find their way home. The coincidences, the people, the books, the resources, and the opportunities will all show up when you're ready and you ask. When the answers come, the inner shift will feel light-filled and miraculous, because it is and so are you.

In my very first yoga class I remember vividly that I could actually feel my feet, almost like I was feeling them for the first time. The feeling was so strong. Like there was no demarcation between the floor and the soles of my feet. I felt grounded, stable, peaceful, energized, and alive, all at the same time. There was no turning back.

I have no idea to this day why yoga popped into my head at such a low part of my life and why I connected the dots to it as a way out of my misery, but somehow, intuitively, instinctively, I knew it was part of the solution. What I didn't know was that it was the answer.

−LORI BERENZ

DO NOT THINK OF YOURSELF AS A
SMALL, COMPRESSED, SUFFERING
THING. THINK OF YOURSELF AS
GRACEFUL AND EXPANDING, NO
MATTER HOW UNLIKELY IT MAY SEEM
AT THE TIME.
−B.K.S. IYENGAR, LIGHT ON LIFE

To Tony and Kyle: words cannot express how much you mean to me.

And to my students, who show up on good days and not so good days. Your commitment, questions, curiosity, passion, and joy inspire me more than you will ever know.

And finally, to all the yogis past and present, the seekers, the searchers, the teachers, and the guides that I have had the pleasure of learning from on my yoga journey, especially B.K.S. Iyengar and his family. Pranam.

LORI BERENZ

Lori Berenz began practicing yoga in 1998 and fell in love with its intensity, discipline, and spirit. Today she is a senior teacher and the director of Yoga Journey, Collingwood. Lori is truly grateful for the gift of yoga and is passionate about sharing this gift with others. Drawing on her own personal experiences, Lori aims to connect with her students on a physical and emotional level. Her classes are fun, inclusive, and engaging, and they are designed for students who want to deepen their practice. In her previous professional life, Lori held management positions in the field of human resources. She is also a mother, a wife, and an advocate for plant-based lifestyles.

@YOGAJOURNEY_COLLINGWOOD

CHAPTER 7:
ON THE PATH TO MY DHARMA

When I was ten, my teacher wrote on my report card that I behaved like "Alice in Wonderland"—(spacey, a daydreamer, disconnected from what was going on around me). Of course, this comment was meant to be a criticism, but I was proud to own that title even while getting scolded by my parents.

More recently I looked up the meaning behind the story of *Alice's Adventures in Wonderland* to find out that it is about an open-minded child's struggle to survive in the confusing world of seemingly nonsensical rule-based adults. Well, that just about sums it up! Although I am now an adult, I still hold onto my "Alice in Wonderland" ethos.

I've always looked at the world with a sense of wonder. Don't get me wrong, this has definitely led me down the garden path at times, but it has also kept me whole and authentically myself. My dad used to refer to me as the "different one" of his three children. I never took this as an insult. I love the fact that he understood me on that level. It's not to say he didn't disagree with me, but he soon realized that it was pointless to try to convince me otherwise when I was bound and determined to do something.

Being the child of immigrants often leads a person to being in a cycle of comparison and needing to work hard to prove oneself. The pressure my parents felt to succeed definitely had an impression on me. I spent the majority of my childhood feeling like I wasn't enough (not pretty enough, thin enough, or smart enough), so I worked hard like my dad did.

Like father, like daughter

Growing up, we had a cottage on a small lake in northern Ontario. My dad built it by himself on a very limited budget. He could only afford to buy so much lumber at a time, so it felt like we stopped at the local lumber store every time we drove up north. He never mentioned the limited budget, I just thought he loved shopping for wood! Trained as a bricklayer but a firefighter by profession, Dad worked multiple construction jobs while I was young, then he'd come home and get changed into his firefighter's uniform and head off to work again.

My dad envisioned this cottage long before it was built. It's like he manifested the cottage into being over a series of several years, and watching him work was like watching someone in meditation. The cottage was an unusual shape with eight sides, like a giant stop sign. It was built in stages, so we lived in a small cabin with no running water while the main cottage was built. I was in my element (except for the real or imagined spiders in the outhouse when I had to go pee in the middle of the night!). We spent every summer there from the last day of school to Labor Day. It was a magical place.

Building this cottage was an act of love for my dad. And because of him, I fell in love with nature. I was completely mesmerized and drawn to the water as a child. I still am, which is why I was drawn to live near the shores of Georgian Bay in Collingwood, Ontario.

Sometimes when I get stressed or anxious, I think about my younger self floating on a raft and looking up at the clouds morphing into various shapes, and it's as if I am there. It's as if I can actually feel the wood that I am lying on, smell the summer breeze, and touch the water. These memories bring me into a state of deep connection with myself and nature. There are no distinctions. We are one.

I drifted away from nature after university, following the pull toward a "real" job. Being self-sufficient was a nonnegotiable for me. From a very young age, I did not want to be dependent on someone else for my well-being. After graduation, I went to college to study human resources and then spent roughly the next fifteen years (minus one blissful period that I spent traveling through Europe) in this profession.

I was good at solving problems and connecting with people and communicating with them. I was also good at cleaning up messes and finding solutions. I didn't fear change and loved a challenge. In one company I was known as the "termination lady" because of the compassion I provided to others during a very difficult time. Often, people I terminated would reach out to me months later and tell me it was the best thing that ever happened to them! I learned a lot from them about accepting and embracing change. All in all, human resources was an interesting profession and provided me with financial independence, but it wasn't my dharma.

Finding yoga

One day I woke up to the realization that I was unhappy. I was a workaholic in a job that didn't fill me up, and I was married to an alcoholic.

Sharing your life with an addict means that you never really know what you're dealing with. You need to be on edge and prepared for anything. Half of the time you walk on eggshells, and half of the time you are on the verge of crying or flying into a rage—at least that was my experience with it.

While my personal life was imploding and I was feeling unfulfilled at work, I was starting to feel the pangs of wanting to become a mother for the first time in my life. Perfect timing! I had reached the point where I would be grocery shopping and would see a child or baby and would be so overcome with emotion that I'd have to leave the store.

So I turned my full attention to work and began succeeding. I got promoted, won the equivalent of the employee of the year award, and was awarded a trip to Japan, but I couldn't escape the inner whisperings of "there's got to be more to life than this." I didn't need to dig too deeply to understand what the voice was trying to say. I had ventured so far away from what made me feel whole and fulfilled that I felt like I was losing myself. I called my mother to ask her about a friend who had traveled to India to study yoga. She got back to me that I needed to attend a certain yoga studio. To this day I remember calling for information and explaining that I had no experience with yoga but was eager to start. The sweet voice said, "Just bring yourself." And so I did.

Back then, yoga tights were not a thing, so I showed up in my neon pink running pants (neon because I used to run at 5 a.m., not because I wanted to stand out in a crowd). When I say I was hooked after my first yoga class, I mean I was hooked! It felt like I had found my people, found myself, and found my home. At the same time, yoga made me feel raw, uncomfortable, and very challenged. It was not at all a gentle awakening, it was more like a solid push. Yoga was like a defibrillator that jolted me out of a dull, insensitive state. From that day forward, I took as many classes and workshops as I could manage. It was the only thing I would leave work for, and it provided me with a safe space from a disintegrating marriage.

In my very first yoga class I remember vividly that I could actually feel my feet, almost like I was feeling them for the first time. The feeling was so strong. Like there was no demarcation between the floor and the soles of my feet. I felt grounded, stable, peaceful, energized, and alive, all at the same time. There was no turning back.

I have no idea to this day why yoga popped into my head at such a low part of my life and why I connected the dots to it as a way out of my misery, but somehow, intuitively, instinctively, I knew it was part of the solution. What I didn't know was that it was the answer.

Eventually, yoga shored me up, gave me confidence, and helped me understand that my marriage was broken and could not be ignored anymore. I informed my husband that I was leaving. As usual, he was emotionally void of any response and seemed not to care too much. I found an apartment close by where we were living, told him I still loved him but could no longer live with him, and moved out. Almost a year later we reconciled, but once again, it crumbled. This time, I knew it was really over and that there was nothing to go back to, so I made a more permanent move by buying a house and in another city. I was committed to moving on.

Life moved forward with a new job in a new town. I had left the broken marriage and had yoga to restore balance and peace. Eventually, I joined a yoga teacher training program. I had no ambition of becoming a yoga teacher, I simply wanted to learn more.

I study and practice Iyengar yoga, known to be the gold standard for yoga teacher training programs. You need to be a student for three years before you can apply to be an apprentice with a teacher. Mentoring can take between three to five years and culminates with a rigorous assessment. I thought, *Cool, I will study and go deep into yoga as I work toward my goal of becoming a vice president of human resources.*

The Universe had different plans for me

One of the relationships I built at work turned out to be something much stronger than collegial. I met my now husband, Tony, the love of my life, at work and decided to resign so he could stay there and we could separate work and love. Our courtship was fast, and I stated very early on that I wanted to have a child. Tony had two boys from his first marriage so he was a little taken aback, but after some consideration he stated that he always wanted more children and was game.

When our son Kyle was about one year old, I returned to work. But with the stress of a toddler and both Tony and me working demanding jobs that required travel, we knew it wasn't sustainable. We discussed options, including me giving up my yoga teaching training, but Tony knew how important that was for me. We decided that Tony would focus on his career and I would start an HR consulting firm and teach yoga on the side while finishing my yoga teacher training.

I traveled to India in 2007 when Kyle was three years old. To this day, one of the most surreal moments of my life was when I arrived at the Iyengar Yoga Institute in Pune and saw B.K.S. Iyengar, one of the world's most influential yogis, in real life. I have been back five times and am looking forward to another visit in the near future. (I never did start that HR consulting business!) Four assessments and almost twenty years of teaching later, I haven't looked back.

In reflection, I realize that so much of my ability to move through difficult times and forward toward change and opportunity hinged on making one decision—one critical, challenging, fear-inducing decision. All I needed to do was ask myself the following questions:

What if I never left that bad marriage?
What if I never left HR?
What if I never married that man?
What if I never had a child?

One night I dreamed about my mother's grandmother in Romania, sitting on a chair, dressed in black, and looking old and weary. She had a message for me: "We went through this so you don't have to. Never keep yourself small. Don't hold back. Be brave and show others how to be brave. Take care of yourself and others. Don't lose yourself like we had to just to survive. You owe this to yourself and to all the other women in our family who came before you."

I realized then that I live a life of extreme privilege. Not in wealth or material possessions, but in freedom—freedom to go to university, to establish a career, to leave a bad marriage, to independently buy a home in my thirties, to embark on a new relationship without recrimination, to have a child in my late thirties, to leave my established career, to pursue my passion for yoga, to experience the transformational effects of yoga in my daily life, and to dream about new adventures and opportunities. I take this privilege seriously and am committed to empowering others to do the same.

I sometimes feel like two different people. There is the person who existed "Before Yoga" and the person that exists "During Yoga" (because I am still in it). However, this feeling, this sensation, is not dualistic, not separate, because the pieces of my life from that point to now have been made whole. They've been stitched together with and through yoga. And through my partner, my child, my friends and family, my home, and my lifestyle.

My husband has always been my biggest supporter. He told me years ago that his initial attraction to me was my intelligence and my ability to connect with others (don't forget, we met at work). His unwavering support comes with a significant commitment of financial support and time, plus an understanding that yoga is the third "person" in our relationship. His ask in exchange for all this support, in consideration of the sacrifices that the family has made for me to pursue this path, is for me to go as far as I can, to continue to study and advance, and not for reasons related to money or status but because he knows how much this form of yoga can help people. Given this, my approach and commitment to yoga has never been a casual one.

Finding joy in doing the work

In order to continue studying, learning, and preparing for yoga teaching assessments, I had to be extremely disciplined. As the mother of a small child, I made the decision to make practice nonnegotiable every day. My son grew up knowing and accepting this expectation. Recently, he has started training for triathlons and said to me, "I was never interested in practicing yoga with you, but I did see how dedicated you were to practicing. When I started becoming interested in participating in triathlons, I knew I had to do the work." Having a child is like turning a mirror onto yourself. The child is the mirror, and you see yourself through them. You see your light side and your shadow side. You can't look away and ignore what is right in front of you, so you have to do the work.

If someone were to ask me what my biggest accomplishment is, without hesitation I would say it is my son. However, there were so many things that came together for my son to evolve from a glimmer of hope into a reality. I fully trust that yoga was this conduit. So essentially, yoga has given me the essence of my life's accomplishment, and my practice continues to be one of my greatest joys. I see my ability to teach the art, science, and philosophy of yoga as a gift beyond measure, and the lessons of running a studio have been significant and challenging.

If I had to describe myself in one word, I would say I am a learner. Just like Alice in Wonderland tried to navigate her way through the confusion of her world, I have spent my life study-ing, observing, and learning. Taking inspiration from the world around me and the tools I have available to me to empower others to own their health and wellness and to embrace the power that lies within—this is my dharma.

Embrace who you are,
reach for that better feeling, stay focused on that big dream,
and enjoy the journey along the way.

−CAITLIN NAGY

THROUGH THE CHALLENGES
I FACED, I DISCOVERED THE
STRENGTH TO STRIVE FOR A LIFE
BEYOND MY WILDEST DREAMS.

*To my mother, Maggi, who taught me the
essence of bravery and the undying spirit of
creativity. And to my daughter, Bridget, my
constant reminder to stand strong and stay
present in every moment.*

CAITLIN NAGY

Caitlin Nagy is a multi-talented creative consultant, excelling in both creative direction and leadership in design. With a remarkable knack for envisioning brand strategies and innovative website designs, she's helping Canadian businesses thrive while prioritizing the wellness of the planet. She has actively connected with an international team, leveraging her expertise to provide strategic creative direction that raises awareness of young onset Parkinson's disease among younger and potentially at-risk demographics. Her impactful contributions have already made a tangible difference in increasing understanding and support for this cause. In her free time, Caitlin finds joy in playful moments with her daughter, indulging in her passion for gardening, and channeling her creative energy into planning her next inspiring project.

@CREATIVEBY_CAITLIN

CHAPTER 8:
CREATING MY DREAM LIFE WHILE NAVIGATING A NEURODEGENERATIVE DISEASE

When you can embrace your storms, you learn so much about yourself and how resilient you truly are. That you are the creator of your own destiny. That you can persevere and fight for a better outcome. That you can create an incredible life that's filled with so much love and happiness.

Life has a funny way of taking unexpected turns. I had a meticulously planned path, focusing on goals and celebrating milestones along the way. I truly believed that with determination and intention, anything was possible. Little did I know that my journey would be reshaped by a formidable opponent: a neurodegenerative disease. But through the challenges I faced, I discovered the strength to strive for a life beyond my wildest dreams.

Like everyone, I've had my fair share of hardships, and I used to find myself caught in a cycle of dwelling on those challenges. There were moments when I would sink into depression, feeling overwhelmed by the weight of my struggles. And then, when I mustered the strength to look beyond them, I would beat myself up for wallowing in that dark place while others seemed to overcome their own obstacles. It took time, but I gradually realized that it wasn't the hardships themselves that defined me, but rather my response to them. I began to view my challenges through a creative lens, finding strength in my perspective and discovering the power to reach for greater heights.

I was thirty-one, I'd just paid off my student debt, and I'd bought my first home with my boyfriend (now husband). Moreover, I had landed the job I had relentlessly pursued. It felt like the realization of a childhood wish, one that had propelled me forward through dark periods in my past—trauma from my childhood in being separated from my mom at a very young age, then losing her to breast cancer right after graduating from high school, my childhood best friend suffering a spinal injury, and the toxic relationships I would jump into to try and escape my reality.

I had finally been able to put all of that behind me. All of the pain and trauma I used as ammo to reach for something better. And I had done it and created the life I had dreamed of—it actually came true! Everything was going to be easy from this point forward . . . happily ever after.

"I had to make you uncomfortable, otherwise you never would have moved." –Universe

Just as life seemed perfect, subtle tremors began to plague my left hand. At first, I dismissed them as minor inconveniences—a pinched nerve, perhaps. But a year later, I received a diagnosis: Parkinsonism. Although genetic testing ruled out Parkinson's disease, the symptoms persisted. The doctors recommended medication and a follow-up in six months. However, deep down,

I couldn't accept this diagnosis. It didn't align with my understanding of Parkinson's as an old person's disease. A fire ignited within me, compelling me to explore alternative therapies for the next six years.

Meanwhile, I was in utter denial and disbelief. I have always trusted my gut, and the whole experience just didn't seem right. And based on my brief consults with doctors, it really felt like there was something that they weren't seeing. I refused to accept the diagnosis. I took matters into my own hands and spent the next six years trying every possible alternative therapy I could find: naturopaths, chiropractors, hypnotherapy, Reiki, IV drip therapy, Farias Dystonia Technique, special diets, expensive supplements—you name it, I have probably tried it.

While alternative therapies didn't replace traditional medication, they were effective in helping me manage the symptoms and delaying going on PD medication. They taught me invaluable lessons about listening to my body, processing trauma, and staying motivated. By age thirty-five, my symptoms progressed, though I managed to conceal them as mere discomfort. Determined to experience motherhood, my husband and I decided to try for a baby.

A lot of the practitioners I had seen over the years said that things would improve if I had a baby. Based on what everybody was saying, I thought I would feel better when I was pregnant. I was so excited to not only be pregnant but also to potentially have the symptoms go away for nine months. But what happened was the opposite. The tremors were in hyper-overdrive, and in each trimester, my symptoms just seemed to get worse. I struggled with major loss of balance and freezing of movement, and I had to be holding on to something to avoid falling down. My husband had to cut my food and cook all my meals for me. I couldn't get dressed on my own.

I was terrified. Things just kept getting worse and worse as the pregnancy progressed, and I was so fearful of how I was going to function being a mom. How was I going to breastfeed and change a diaper? Would I be able to pick up the baby? It was so scary and so depressing.

Surprisingly, I had the easiest delivery I could have ever imagined, especially after the pain I'd experienced during my pregnancy. And I delivered a beautiful baby girl after a short labor.

So here I was. I had gotten everything that I had always wanted. Except my body just wasn't caught up to what I had planned for my life.

Being a new mom is not easy, especially without your own mom to comfort and guide you. And when you're living with health issues that take away your ability to perform what should be simple tasks, there is a whole other level of "not easy." I was terrified about how I was going to handle it. Picking her up and learning how to breastfeed was so scary. Holding her and being afraid I'd drop her was hard.

I quickly fell into postpartum depression and encountered many moments when I felt like it would be easier for everyone if I ended my life. It got to the point that when I breastfed, I would have a huge tremor, leg cramping, the sweats, and paralysis. Every day felt like it was Groundhog Day; I'd be drenched in sweat and crying. I couldn't pick up my daughter without someone helping me. I couldn't walk across the room or even sit up on my own.

But in those dark and terrifying moments of despair, a gentle yet confident voice from deep inside kept saying, "Fight for it. Find the solution. Live your life." So I stopped myself right there. All the work I had done on myself, everything I had tackled and achieved, everything that I had manifested in my life—I had created that. And this uncontrollable crazy thing that was happening to me, that no one around me understood, that had totally moved me off course on what I had planned for my life—it clearly wasn't going anywhere. If anything, it kept getting louder and louder. So there wasn't anything else to do but accept it, be patient with it, and trust that everything was happening for a reason.

I had made it all happen. I had spent five years so focused on my health, so I decided that I was going to heal my body. I was going to get better. And that needed to start with looking at this monster that had taken over my life, staring straight at it and calling it for what it was: Parkinson's Disease.

So I decided to start taking the medication.

I remember the day when my body finally started to feel the meds kick in. It was such a high for me. I could walk around the room without limping, and my left arm didn't shake. I had a full-on dance party in my office that day, just jumping around for a solid two hours. It was like being reborn again. It felt so amazing.

But the medication wasn't a magic elixir; it came with some pretty shitty side effects like dyskinesia, a condition characterized by involuntary, abnormal, and often repetitive movements. It can affect various parts of the body, including the face, limbs, and trunk. And it literally makes you twitch and wiggle like you're a meth addict. As if freezing and shaking weren't enough, try going out in public or leading a client meeting while having a dyskinesia attack. Yeah, that brings in a whole new level of humbleness.

Let me tell you about the wild ride that comes with taking medication for Parkinson's disease. Brace yourself because it's a roller coaster of precise timing and protein restrictions. You see, the meds only work their magic for a mere two to three hours, but there's a catch. You've got to pop that pill thirty minutes before you even think about devouring some protein. And if you accidentally chow down on a juicy steak too soon, well, kiss the rest of your day goodbye.

But wait, there's more! Ladies, listen up because this one's for you. The medication behaves differently inside our female bodies. Just when you think you've got it figured out, ovulation and menstruation swoop in and wreak havoc. It's like a symphony of side effects and mood swings that no one warned us about. Can you believe that over 85 percent of women with Parkinson's experience changes in symptoms and medication effects throughout our cycles? It's mind-boggling!

Now, here's a mind-blowing fact for you. The hormones in a woman's brain can fluctuate by a whopping 25 percent during each cycle. You'd think this would raise some eyebrows in those fancy movement disorder clinics, but nope, it's often overlooked. And get this—Canada's "gold standard" treatment for women with PD, Levodopa, was designed with men's brains in mind. We're talking about a treatment approach that hasn't evolved since the groovy 1960s. Can you believe it? I sure can't!

But don't worry, I've got a glimmer of hope to share with you. I truly believe we've stumbled upon an untapped opportunity for Parkinson's treatment here. If this book manages to bring a brilliant neurologist together with a badass female reproductive hormone specialist, we might just have a chance at a breakthrough. Imagine the possibilities when these two powerhouses join forces! It's time to shake things up, challenge the status quo, and revolutionize how we approach and tackle this sneaky disease.

Fast-forward to now, and it's been nine years since my symptoms started. There are good days and there are bad days, and then there are really horrible ones when I have no other choice but to listen to my body, rest, and be present and think about all of the wonderful things happening around me. It has taught me a lot about how to love the things I hated most about myself and embrace the journey I have been given. When I can be present with whatever storm I'm in and get into a state of gratitude for all the amazing things in my life, I can embrace the pain and use it as a launch pad to create amazing things.

With a newfound acceptance and a surge of energy coursing through me, I shed the shame I'd carried and embraced my diagnosis as part of who I am. This shift opened doors to connection and vulnerability. Sharing my story allowed others to open up, creating a support network where experiences were shared and strength was found. In understanding the struggles of others, I realized that we are all fighting our own battles, and together, we lift each other higher.

This gave me an entirely new perspective on my life and all that I had accomplished, plus a thirst to achieve more and enjoy my life to the fullest. I'm a mom and I steer my own career path, leading several teams and managing four different businesses. My only wish is that I knew that there was hope earlier on, which is why I want other people with young onset Parkinson's and neurodegenerative conditions to know that they are not alone. This is not the end. And the louder our voices are, the more people will listen. And if you are a woman who has been newly diagnosed with YOPD, be ready to advocate for yourself. Don't downplay your symptoms. TRACK them! And make sure you continue to show your doctor the reports.

My hope with sharing my story is that it will motivate other women who might be battling within themselves and their bodies to not be ashamed. Embrace who you are, reach for that better feeling, stay focused on that big dream, and enjoy the journey along the way.

Even when we're not actively looking to make a decision,
life is unfolding for us.

—AMANDA JEROME

WHILE FATE MAY PLAY A ROLE
IN OUR LIVES, WE STILL HAVE THE
FREE WILL TO MAKE CHOICES AND
SHAPE OUR DESTINY.

*To those who encouraged me to take the leaps, this
is for you. And to those who tried to hold me back,
this is for me. To my sons and my stars who remind
me to—and join me in—pause and play.*

AMANDA JEROME

Amanda Jerome is an award-winning wedding producer and CEO of The Wedding Society. Her thirty years of experience in hospitality and events is rich with deep-rooted community connections. Amanda is passionate about bringing together local businesses that are dedicated to being an all-inclusive resource for couples as they collectively promote destination weddings throughout Canadian tourism regions. Amanda is also the publisher of local wedding guide publications. She resides in Collingwood, Ontario, with her husband, two children, a pup, and parents. She enjoys dinner with "framily" and is fascinated by love and champagne.

@AMANDAJEROMEEVENTS @GEORGIANBAYWEDDING
@THEWEDDINGSOCIETY.CA @WEDDINGPLANNING101.CA

CHAPTER 9:
FATE VERSUS FREE WILL

The journey to seek my truth has led me to follow anything that brings me joy. There has been a constant theme of accepting my path and what has led me to where I am today as fate. Or have I had the free will to change, influence, and control moments and outcomes in life? Quite possibly it's both, in a forever spar of seemingly friendly, sometimes unfriendly, blows.

I've struggled to come up with just one decision that has brought me to where I am today. My story is a culmination of little choices mixed with some really big ones, along with moments that didn't feel like a choice at all. It's the feeling of having lived a thousand lifetimes in one and trying to tell the story of how they all fit together.

The questions of "Am I enough?", "Am I doing this right?", and "Did I make the right decision?" haunt me. Despite the nagging limiting beliefs, every day I move the needle a touch further. Even days when I'm frozen with fear bring me closer to a project completion, as it allows me to slow down, reflect, rest, and reset before the forward motion slingshot.

I tend to find myself asking for permission in every decision I make, in every idea I have. But that permission is something that exists within me, something I don't need to have someone else give me. Looking back on some of my biggest growth moments in my life, as much as there were decisions, they were obvious no-brainers. They were always meant to be. There were passive moments and action-taking moments. Realizing what I do have control over has provided me with a deeper understanding and appreciation for the things I have zero control over.

In retrospect, I was always meant to become an entrepreneur. As a child, my most peaceful moments and cherished core memories were spent organizing my closet and filing school projects. Making loads of friends and being a part of large social groups wasn't my jam, and I often felt out of place trying too hard to belong. Through high school, a passion for photography began as I felt a deep connection with capturing moments of joy, sadness, and fleeting teenage Friday nights; it was a way to hold on to moments that I didn't want to let go of.

Growing up in suburban Ottawa, then moving to the small town of Thornbury with fewer than 2,000 people, gave me very little opportunity to discover much more than my first jobs in hospitality. As far as industry went in this small town, as a teen, you were either going to work in the bank, on a farm, or at one of ten restaurants. Dad was a banker, and no way was I getting muddy, so restaurants it was. Hospitality has always been a part of me, like breathing. As a child, I loved setting the perfect table only to watch everyone gather, socialize, debate, laugh, and be in the moment. Watching my grandmother, aunts, and mother spend endless hours in the kitchen preparing feasts is where my most treasured memories belong. We were often in the kitchen prepping, cooking, or cleaning, and I couldn't imagine being anywhere else. It was no surprise that my first jobs were working as a counter girl in the local bakery, then dishwashing and cooking, and later serving at many of the local restaurants.

In an effort to move away from the known, to grow and do different things, I chose to forgo university with friends, and after high school, I traveled to California to follow my childhood dream. In youth, we take risks without perceived rewards. My goal at this young age was to settle in, grow my roots, become a state citizen, go to university, and live happily ever after with my first love. There's no surprise that this adventure was short-lived. No matter how far you go, whatever you try to run away from will follow. Heartbroken, I had no sense of free will in this moment as fate whisked me back home to be faced with the "what next" of life while dealing with the deep sense of failure I felt from not realizing that goal at nineteen.

Mental health struggles in my generation were taboo and never really something I understood until my twenties, although it affected every aspect of my life from my youth to this day. Never having the sense of self-confidence or knowing what a boundary was left me feeling alone, lonely, and not wanting to be in my own skin. In fact, as a young teen, I would attempt at scraping the skin off my arms, as the physical pain seemed to somehow release my mental anguish. It wasn't until I was faced with the sudden death of a friend right before the year 2000 that I was set on the course to healing my inner wounds. I worked toward stepping out of the victim mentality and focused on personal betterment, becoming obsessed with it, learning what it meant to allow joy, positivity, and gratitude into my life. I decided then that I had the freedom to not allow myself the fate of depression, sadness, bitterness, and gloom. I met a therapist, started taking meds for anxiety and depression, and felt worse than I had when I started.

The path of mental health and freedom from my own drowning thoughts is a constant journey, and it's a continual choice to not be consumed by them. I've done everything from different styles of therapy to medication to omitting dietary intolerances. Most recently, I've been learning more about the disconnect between our physical body and spiritual body and how to get them to speak to one another through something as simple as breathing. Every choice I've made to understanding my fate, not accepting anything that doesn't bring joy and happiness into my life, and being patient with the tests of the universe along my path has brought me to the now.

I still have personal judgments, criticisms, and limiting beliefs. I can hear the negative voice within. It's come from holding me so far back to reminding me to sink a little deeper within myself to ask the hard questions. Is it true? Where is this coming from? Is there anything I can do about it right now? Yet I can be so immersed in my light, in my heart-centered purpose when I'm not thinking about it. Don't think, just do.

Who defines one's purpose anyway? One may comment that it's those we surround ourselves with who give us clues to define it. Or perhaps it's our lineage and path set out by our parents and ancestors. I have always had a burning desire to understand "why I have to do life this way." Asking this question has provided me with options, and options give opportunities that lead to more aligned decisions in life.

In university, I took a little time exploring what my core interest was. Fascinated with people, I began my path with psychology, which I combined with business and marketing to get an overview of the business of humans and their exchanges. I graduated during the recession in 2003, and when no one was hiring, I felt lost on my path once again. Not wanting to go back to where I had come but instead looking for new paths to walk, I moved into a little apartment in Collingwood, Ontario, and began a job in hospitality again, where I began climbing the ladder from management to catering director to event planning.

In 2007, I began working at a local golf club. Having never even been to a wedding before, I was frozen with fear when the first inquiry to host a wedding at the golf club came across my desk. Without choice, I dove into the experience with much trial and error and never looked back. I was obsessed and felt I had landed into a job that I could really sink into. My mental health was finally in a stable place, my physical health was never better after focusing on dietary cleanses and better habits, and I couldn't get enough of my job. And with a cherry on top, that fall, after my first year of weddings, I met my forever love.

I spent the majority of my twenties and thirties in learning mode, making huge mistakes in relationships and lifestyle habits, second-guessing myself at any opportunity, and soaking up any joyful moment I could hold on to. My career path during this time led me to absorbing and exploring business management methods, education, and practices. Learning most of what I didn't want to be a part of along the way.

There's always been drive, passion, and ambition deep within me, innately. I come from a lineage of hardworking men and stronger women. As I continued down my multi-job path, I found myself in jobs that were quite autonomous, and I thrived in those for a time. From small business to corporate jobs, there were glaring challenges of being a strong and heart-centered woman among the status quo. I was often labeled as sensitive and emotional. The climate of business is quite masculine focused. I experienced and watched the heart of it all get lost along the way to chasing dollars. But I later discovered that chasing what lights up your heart keeps you aligned with your purpose and that's what attracts money. I quickly found I out-grew jobs, and the ones I felt qualified for, I grew out of fastest. Jobs I took to learn from took me to the point of expansion, then quickly to the point of stress, pain, and exhaustion. That was a clear sign to me that I needed a change: the moment I found myself getting sucked into the vortex of misery instead of following my joy, passion, and purpose.

After work at the golf club one evening, one of my best friends and I chatted about the future as we planned our weddings together. She and her fiancé had been planning a destination wedding, while my fiancé and I had chosen to stay local. As we discussed ideas, I realized the limited options available in our area, which led me to researching various private spaces and vendors that serviced the region beyond the scope of what I had been introduced to and using in my current job. That lit my fire. If I was looking for this as a venue coordinator for wed-dings, then think of all the other engaged couples who'd need help! The Georgian Bay Wedding Society was born, a robust community of local wedding professionals—a one-stop shop for couples planning their wedding in South Georgian Bay. What began as a thirty-page booklet with eight advertisers has grown in thirteen years to a 130+ page guide with over 80+ society members, and expansion throughout tourism regions in Ontario and Canada has already begun.

Even when we're not actively looking to make a decision, life is unfolding for us.

The next step toward falling deeper into weddings was when my youngest son was born and I had just started a new job. There were limitations to when I could book weddings at the venue I was working at, and my husband said, "Why don't you advertise yourself as a wedding planner in your own magazine?" My immediate response was hesitancy. Weddings usually take place on Saturdays, which was my family time. The kids were young and the marriage strained from working long shifts opposite one another. With my husband's encouragement, I put myself out there and the advertising worked. I booked my first wedding, and the years that followed only came with more requests for planning services. The idea of quitting the corporate job to go out on my own had been discussed before, but it was hard to give up perceived financial security.

On July 7, 2018, I was working a wedding for my "day" job and had another wedding that same day through my "side hustle" with one of my associates running that event. All day, I couldn't shake the thought that I was working at the wrong event and was meant to be at the other wedding. When I got home that night, I was finally able to get my thoughts together and present the idea to my husband for me to quit my job and go out on my own. It was truly something I should have done long before, but the timing never felt right. Timing is everything, and I received the permission I thought I needed. More importantly, I gave myself the permission to no longer work for someone else.

Two years later, I was living the entrepreneur dream and had a sweet taste of the excitement and potential success to come, until fate stepped in with our global pandemic halting all events, weddings, and human contact. Although we as humanity were all going through it as one, our individual experiences made it feel scary and isolating.

The pandemic also brought with it an opportunity to slow down, to get real about how I was living my life in high gear, and wow, did that ever put a spotlight on what that stress was doing to my family, let alone to my own personal health and well-being. It was a once-in-a-lifetime chance to pause amid the chaos of motherhood and solo-prenuership, which opened wounds I had thrown bandages on over the years as I focused on raising two boys, running two businesses, and keeping a marriage intact. The sense of how out of touch with myself I was got placed under the magnifying glass.

Fate swung around again, dredging up recurring patterns of mental health issues. The couples I was working with got the very best of what was left of me as my heart broke over and over for more than forty couples who either canceled or postponed their celebrations. What was left of me for my family, or even for me? Realizing how much of my identity was wrapped up in what I was doing for others, I decided that enough was enough. I missed my family, I missed my friends, and I really missed me!

Although the pandemic forced us away from one another physically, it brought a chance to connect with people in a new old-fashioned way, and it gave us a chance to get in touch with ourselves again. I made a choice to start showing up for me in ways I hadn't before.

My family means everything to me, but without learning to prioritize my own needs, I was nothing to those around me. Through making new friendships and connections, I was inspired to try business differently, and most importantly, to start seeing myself as the successful entrepreneur I already was. I began investing in myself beyond traditional education and joined The Monarch & Co. I had always had the dream of expanding The Wedding Society beyond the Georgian Bay region, and I formulated the foundations in making that expansion happen and reassess my event company to prepare for the biggest wedding years in history when the world finally reopened.

One thing that has kept me in entrepreneurship is the community of women that I've met both within my industry and outside of it. It's also me being open to meeting new people, letting down the walls, and trusting these new experiences as opportunities. Through gatherings and workshops, my network of women entrepreneurs grew exponentially, and the power of collaboration and community grew even stronger. I finally felt a sense of belonging among other heart-centered people who celebrated this characteristic. The feeling of investing in

ME was freeing. I let go of any mom guilt of not putting all my hard-earned money right back into the family and realized that my self-investment has returns beyond my wildest dreams.

Working with my personal coach over the last two years has been life changing. My goals have manifested faster than ever and my business revenue doubled from 2021 to nearly a half a million in 2022. Through giving myself the credit I deserved, it opened my mind to learning what it meant to ask for help. It didn't mean I was failing and couldn't do it on my own, it meant I didn't have to do it alone and that all my dreams could come true even faster. Just my luck, I had the right people to help build this team: incredible women I had been working alongside and mentoring. My teams are built by personalizing their jobs to suit them and their talents. By leaning into what brings us joy, we get the job done with staggering efficiency and success.

Every decision I have ever made has placed me in my present moment. The hardest part, yet so far the most rewarding and exciting, has been learning who I am, what lights me up, and what brings me overflowing surreal joy. Entrepreneurship feels big—so does prioritizing my goals and finding my own alignment with the world. Taking steps to explore different ways of thinking and seeing life outside of what I was raised to believe brings me closer to who I'm meant to be. Working with a phenomenal hypnotherapist, I was able to release limiting core beliefs that have been holding me back in life—things that didn't even belong to me, and it was time to set them free. Mindset development was the key to unlocking my true fate.

Our role as humans is to explore what is presented to us on our path through life and experience it. Let it in, process it, let it go. We are not born with fear or insecurities. There are ancestral traumas and childhood experiences that stick with us and shape our interactions with the world. There is fear to move forward, and we often snap right back into our comfort zones, bad habits, and negative thought patterns. Finally learning how to override my monkey mind and healing these traumas is the rocket launcher to where I am today. I'm still not sure what I'm meant to be, but I know I'm not meant to be small. I've learned that I don't have anything to prove to anyone, not even myself. There is a driving force behind our decisions, but understanding the why will often help us sift through the nonsense. Healthy boundaries help us make aligned decisions. Anytime you make a choice that benefits you, it's the right one, as it benefits everyone around you. The more focus that's put on this goal, the healthier your boundaries will be.

While fate may play a role in our lives, we still have the free will to make choices and shape our destiny. I believe that hard work and determination have played a significant role in my success, and I feel grateful for the opportunities I've had and for the encouragement from my dear family and friends who could see things in me that I couldn't. When I made the decision to show up for me with unconditional love, everything changed.

I wouldn't have met all these beautiful versions of myself over the years if I hadn't had the courage to follow my gut and my heart all those years ago.

−VANESSA LOCICERO

IT WAS THE COURAGE TO GO FOR IT IN
SPITE OF THE UNKNOWNS AND THE FEAR
THAT OTHERS MIGHT NOT UNDERSTAND
THAT MADE EACH PIVOT I TOOK POSSIBLE.

*This chapter is dedicated to the young woman I was
when I finally let my courage win over my fear.*

VANESSA LOCICERO

Vanessa Locicero is the Soul Attorney™. A chef turned lawyer, entrepreneur and law firm owner, Vanessa infuses a heart-centered approach with the law to support business owners with getting Legally Lit to help them feel educated and empowered using legal strategies to protect themselves and their businesses from risk. Her journey has been full of big pivots, but it's in those transitional moments when she's gained the most clarity and momentum.

@SOUL.ATTORNEY

CHAPTER 10:
FROM THE KITCHEN TO THE COURTROOM

I was twenty-one years old, sitting on an old ratty chair in my bright yellow university apartment with my roommate, Anja, and feeling so lost with the direction of my life when I made the decision that would change the trajectory of my entire life and set me off on a journey of deep self-discovery and actualization. It was the decision to be courageous in the face of fear, expectations, and unfulfillment.

I went to a great university and studied political science and religious studies. I was always an A student, "classified" as "gifted" from a young age, and relished life as an overachiever. I grew up participating in music lessons for various instruments, public speaking, and theater. I was captain of the rugby and wrestling teams and was on the student council. People in my life expected I would continue the path directly from undergrad to law school and go on to be a brilliant attorney because, as they said, I have the "gift of the gab."

In the summer before my final year of university, I wrote the LSAT for the first time, the test one must take before applying to law school. It was expected of me. It was part of the "plan." I had taken an LSAT prep course and hated every minute of it. That summer I'd been playing the tenor saxophone in the house band for a comedy show and had no interest in even thinking about law. Plus, the other students in the LSAT course and the vibe of the teacher really rubbed me the wrong way. Needless to say, I bombed the test.

After my epic failure of an attempt at the LSAT, I had one final year of undergrad left, and while I saw everyone else around me making decisions about where to go next in their educational or career journeys, I had no idea what I wanted for my life.

Growing up in my family as a second-generation Italian immigrant, I saw my fair share of successful business owners and professionals in addition to happy people working in jobs for other companies. I didn't have a good sense back then of the different types of opportunities that were available to me, and I felt really boxed in by a few narrow choices for my next steps.

Thankfully, the Universe aligned me with my best friend since first year, Anja, who was a drama and theater major, and brought the yin to my yang. During the last months of that final year of university, Anja and I stayed up late many nights talking about life and about the future. We developed such a deep bond that I was able to be vulnerable with her about where I was in life. I had been struggling on and off with depression for a few years during that time, and the purposelessness and lack of direction I felt left me like a ship without a rudder, spinning in circles.

All Anja and I knew was that when I got home from late nights working and studying at the library, I would cook. And my oh my, the food that came out of our tiny galley kitchen in our second-floor apartment was mouthwatering and the true definition of comfort food. Anja had read an article about a chef in Spain, Ferran Adrià, whose restaurant, El Bulli, had been voted Best Restaurant in the World and was creating molecular gastronomy magic (before that was a "thing"). She showed me the article, and after reading about the passion and creativity that were possible in the culinary world, I was enthralled.

During that fateful conversation when Anja and I were talking about life after school, she suggested that I go to culinary school instead of grad school. It was such an expansive idea that it blew me out of the water. I felt the weight of the expectations of others leave my body when she introduced the idea.

That decision had ripple effects on every facet of the rest of my life. Choosing to follow my passion for cooking and what made my heart sing rather than what I had been programmed to want from a young age was the journey my heart needed to go on to get to where I am today.

My time spent in culinary school, in professional kitchens and hotels, and in the hospitality industry was exactly the perspective I needed in my life. I learned so much about hard work, working with a team under high-stress circumstances, and what it means when the "buck" actually stops with you. Cooking gave me the opportunity to live in Banff, Alberta, where I worked as a chef at the Fairmont Hotel in Lake Louise. I fell in love with the mountains and met new friends who expanded my perspective on spirituality that would forever change my deepest understanding of the Universe in a way that studying religious studies in university never could. I started reading books about quantum physics, energy, epigenetics, and spirituality. I started exploring crystals, past-life regression, energy healing, and oracle cards. I felt a deep calling to these practices as part of the bigger picture, but I never knew how the soulful and spiritual side of my passion fit into my journey other than as something to support me along my path.

While I continued to excel and had some incredible opportunities, that feeling of "this isn't quite working for me" started creeping up again. I loved the work, but I hated the idea of cooking someone else's recipes and having no say in the creativity or vision; I dreamed up menus that I would have at my own restaurant one day.

The desire to become my own boss and chart my own course was instilled in me at a young age. My father was a self-made man, and I grew up watching people make their own schedules, so being told by a boss where to be and when always grated on me. My dad never fit into the box and always did things his way. He had the courage to choose himself, and he'd say to me, "It's better to be alone than in bad company." That lesson stands the test of time.

How to get from A to B?

But I had a problem. After a four-year honors degree and a two-year diploma in culinary business management and work experience, I still had no idea how to get from A to B. *How does one even start a business?* I often thought. *Who do I need to know to make this happen?* So, like the self-proclaimed nerd in me, I started reading and researching. I wanted to have the tools to know how to start my own business, and I also realized that if I could learn how to do it maybe I could help other people do it too. I had a newfound reason and actual purpose to attend law school. I wanted to become a "food lawyer," but what I didn't know at the time was that a food lawyer is really a business lawyer who helps food businesses.

I'm not going to take you through the whole process of getting into law school and what that part of the journey was about. That'll require an entire book (so stay tuned!). What I will say is that I had to muster up the courage to pivot from the culinary world back into the world of academics. This required a mindset shift that, truthfully, I had a hard time making. I felt like a fish out of water back in school, and I had to take action every day to get my head in the right mindset in order to crush through the mental barriers that were making my dreams drown in impostor syndrome. I started listening to affirmations, sometimes multiple times a day. They helped remind me about the good things and new ways of thinking about myself and the world that I wanted to align with. Over the years it's transitioned to being an annual energetic reset where I record a meditation in my own voice that I listen to in the mornings when I get ready that helps me align with my goals for the upcoming year. Some may say "nuts," others say "smart."

While I was in law school, I dove headfirst into any and every business law course I could fit into my schedule. I took the Canadian Securities course on top of my course load during one of my hardest semesters so I could know about the markets and financial sector and have that inform my legal perspective. I loved it so much that I competed in a cross-Canada mock-trial competition for corporate law and placed second individually in the competition.

As law school was coming to a close, I found myself with a job for my articles, a ten-month internship a law school graduate has to complete before being "called to the bar." It was with a commercial litigation firm in downtown Toronto with excellent and cut-throat attorneys who go hard and win big for their clients. I had always wanted to be a downtown lawyer, like Miranda from *Sex and the City*, so I was shocked when that feeling of "this doesn't feel right" started to sink in halfway through my articles. So, after months of debate, I answered the call and made the decision to leave downtown practice and move to a place that had a different approach. People questioned me for abandoning my budding legal career to move up north to "cottage country" to start my legal career, but something inside of me knew it was the right thing to do. I wanted to take the risk for myself and my own quality of life.

I spent the first four years of practice working in commercial and civil litigation in Barrie, Ontario, and Collingwood, Ontario, before realizing yet again that something about it wasn't working. Lawyers dealing with lawsuits always have clients going through something upsetting and challenging, and they are bound by what they can offer them by what remedies are available in the courts. This doesn't always end with "justice" or "fairness" and can often cost tens of thousands of dollars and several years of your life. So at the last firm I worked for, I started transitioning my work over to a more transactional practice. I educated and advised clients who were at the beginning of the process and helped them so that they could avoid potential problems; I started drafting wills and contracts and helping people set up companies. However, this work made me feel too micromanaged, and after one annoying email too many, I decided I'd had enough with the life of an employee and always having to follow someone else's process and procedure.

I wanted to go solo and start my own firm, but I didn't have a plan. So, I just jumped. It was scary to be my own boss in the beginning: I had no one to point to if something happened; I had only myself to rely on to bring in money and clients; I had to manage my finances, schedule, and workflow. But now, I help people just like me who want to start businesses, and I make sure they are legally protected so they can focus on their craft and making money. Not only do I provide traditional legal services under my law firm banner, Locicero Legal PC, but I also mentor and educate business owners on important legal topics through my course Legally Lit, offer private mentorship, and host Legal Eats dinners. I even built an online legal template library where entrepreneurs can get access to the legal contracts they need to do business at a fraction of the price working with a lawyer one-to-one. I love how I get to be a lawyer—how I get to show up as myself in my brand, in my marketing, for my clients and for my community, again and again, even when it might be contrary to the expected "way" of doing things.

I've learned that having the courage to embrace my whole self and be vulnerable and share that woman with the world is the way I connect with the people and clients who love to work with me. And I love to work with them. If I'm "too much," "too loud," or "too weird" for you, then you're probably not my people, and that's okay.

It was the courage to go for it in spite of the unknowns and the fear that others might not understand that made each pivot I took possible. I have been told that I'm an "old soul" and that I've "lived many lifetimes" in my years so far, and I do feel fortunate to say that I think I have. I wouldn't have met all these beautiful versions of myself over the years if I hadn't had the courage to follow my heart and my stomach toward my culinary career all those years ago, or if I didn't have the courage to continue to listen to the whispers of my soul and to what my gut tells me moment by moment. It wouldn't have been possible if I didn't have the courage to accept myself as a changing creature throughout different phases in life and to push myself outside of my own comfort zones toward goals that make me feel excited.

Pursuing your passion takes courage

If there's one thing I've learned since making that very first big decision it's that pursuing your passions in life takes courage, determination, and a whole lot of grit. It takes choosing you, over and over again. That's what I used as my compass amid all the twists and turns and pivots in the process: my intuition. There will always be people or circumstances outside of you that you want to do something for or expectations you want to meet for others. It takes courage to say no to those expectations and to show up for what you believe in even when you're scared, when you're the only person in the room you know. It takes courage to build relationships with others and be vulnerable enough so that you can open yourself up to support from the Universe.

I am still working on giving up the martyr complex, the belief that I have to give up myself in order to give to the greater good. I'm working on remaining committed to filling my own cup on a day-to-day basis. It's hard when my type A personality goes a million miles a minute, but I have to realize I created this life to have freedom, not to shackle myself with even more. The lesson of "making my needs known" has been a repeating lesson that I'm still working on getting because it hasn't seemed to stick just yet. I'm not perfect, nor do I ever want to be, but I know that I can sleep well at night knowing I had the "lady balls" to live life according to my own rules and put the insecure impostor to rest for good.

As women, we do so much for other people that it can be easy to lose sight of what we really want to be and how we want to live. Have the courage to choose yourself over and over again. To pursue freedom in whatever way it looks to you. To take the road less traveled—or to trail blaze your own path if need be. To be committed to this path in your deepest soul. To be different and love yourself more because of it.

The world needs what you have. That thing inside of you that doesn't seem to go away.

In the moments of fear or despair, trust in yourself and know that you can accomplish anything if you just have courage.

YOU are more powerful than you realize . . . YOU hold all the answers you seek . . . YOU are the key to your freedom. Every experience you navigate in life is an opportunity to open, soften, and deepen your capacity for love, joy, presence, peace, and connection. Trust your heart—it knows the way.

—EDIE GUDAITIS

I REALIZED THAT I WAS THE COMMON PIECE IN ALL MY EXPERIENCES— THE AWESOME MOMENTS AND THE SHITTY ONES—AND ONLY I COULD CHANGE MY LIFE FOR THE BETTER . . . SO I DID.

To my family and my friends. Thank you for teaching me about love and for encouraging me to trust my intuition.

EDIE GUDAITIS

Edie Gudaitis is the owner of Edie Gudaitis Wellness. She is a Stress Management + Grief Coach, Yoga + Meditation Instructor, and a Breathwork Facilitator. Edie is the creator of various online programs that help people process heavy emotions, navigate grief, and reduce stress. She leads workshops and retreats as well as creates workplace wellness programs that help to reduce employee burnout and turnover. Edie is an advocate for accessible health and wellness programming and is passionate about educating communities on stress, grief, and nervous-system regulation.

@EDIEGUDAITIS.WELLNESS
WWW.EDIEGUDAITISWELLNESS.COM

CHAPTER 11:
TRUST YOUR HEART—
IT KNOWS THE WAY

Sometimes I wonder who I'd be and how my life would feel if moments had unfolded differently and I'd made other decisions.

We are always one decision away from living the life of our dreams. One decision, that's all. Yet when fear takes hold, that one decision is suppressed, and MANY other decisions take our attention away from our heart, our truth, and our presence.

Cultivating self-awareness

We are constantly making decisions to feel safe within ourselves and within the moment—to feel or not feel emotions, to do or not do things, to open and connect with others, or to numb out and shut down. These decisions are so subtle that often we don't realize we are making them—Every. Single. Second—until we get curious about ourselves. Until we turn our awareness within and slow down to a pace where we can actually witness our thoughts and actions instead of being absorbed into the drama of them all. I began to trust the nudges of my intuition and make decisions that ultimately led me on "my path" in the spring of 2008. That is when my story of courage and love began.

I was first introduced to yoga in early 2008 at a YMCA Flow class. Something in my heart stirred as I moved through the practice. There was a curiosity and a peacefulness that I hadn't experienced in my performative dance background. Dance had brought me joy, and it also brought me stress as I tried to mold myself into the tight framework of how a ballet dancer "looks" and "moves." When I first attended yoga classes, I was performative and critical of myself (like I was in the dance classes), but I noticed a gentleness within me surfacing too.

Time travel to October 2014 when I was living in Whistler, British Columbia. I admitted I was unhappy, my health was not great, and I'd finally agreed to see a therapist. I was navigating worsening digestive issues, I was on various elimination diets, and I'd made the decision to move back to my parents (in Ontario) the next month to gain further support as I sought more answers to understand, and improve, my increasing health issues. I remember feeling anger, distrust, and shame toward my body. I worked out at the gym to process the anger, or I drank too much when I went out to bars with friends to numb the discomfort and "feel free" in the moment. It was a dark time in my life. A close friend finally got through to me and emphasized that I needed help.

The next day I met with an outreach worker at Whistler Community Services Society, and within minutes of chatting, I fell apart. The tears kept flowing as I began to admit the truth of how I felt. And beneath the tears came a desire to better understand myself, to reconnect with my body, and to cultivate self-love.

The desire to feel ALIVE, to be present, and to feel happier and stronger guided me back to my yoga practice. Within a few classes, I KNEW I wanted to get certified and teach. I LOVED the way I felt after each practice and loved the beauty, power, and ease that each teacher I practiced with embodied.

Within a month of moving home to my parents, I had an over-whelming feeling that I needed to be back in Whistler. So after only two months in Ontario, I moved back. I was at work when I got the call. It felt surreal and shocking, but not surprising. At that moment, I knew why I felt the pull to move back—I was SO grateful I'd followed the nudge from my heart.

After recovering from a few severe concussions sustained in early 2014, my sister had begun experiencing frequent and painful headaches that fall and winter. I knew something was up. In January 2015, she experienced stroke-like symptoms and was taken to the ER in Whistler. I rushed over as soon as I received the call. When I arrived at her side, I made another decision: to stay and to be strong. I knew that's what she would do if it were me in her shoes. And I knew that's what my parents needed too.

Within minutes of being at the Whistler Medical Clinic, a nurse came to inform me that a helicopter was on the way to bring my sister to Vancouver General Hospital (VGH). I had twenty minutes to go home and pack a bag for my sister and me before catching the helicopter. I was vibrating from shock and fear. I wanted to curl up into a ball under a big warm blanket. I wanted to blink and have her be healthy again. But something within me chose to lean in and stay present.

When we got to VGH, I did the same. I spoke with the doctors, I collected information, I relayed it to our parents, and I stayed by her side. When my mom arrived the next day, having not slept and looking frightened as shit, I stayed. I chose to be the rock. I made the decision to be brave, to anchor into the strength, courage, and the wisdom of my heart instead of drowning in fear. After a few tests, my sister was diagnosed with a very brutal case of viral meningitis. Within a week she was discharged from the NICU floor and returned home to Whistler. It was a slow recovery, but she is now healthy and thriving.

The power of my intuition

The experience reminded me of the power of my intuition, highlighted the fragility of life, and emphasized the importance of making the most of it. Courage, love, and a desire for a deeper understanding of my truth is the thread that connects every "one decision" that has followed since and led me to who and where I am now.

A month after the experience with my sister, I felt another nudge from my heart. It was a whisper to go to Hawaii, Costa Rica, or Bali to complete my 200-hour yoga teacher training (YTT). Since November 2014, I'd been diving deeper into my yoga practice, mindfulness, and self-awareness. It felt like I was waking up to something and also coming home. When I heard the whisper to do my YTT, I remember feeling a lightning bolt of energy dance through my body as if THIS WAS MY PATH. It felt so right, so in alignment, even though it didn't make any sense. Excited to follow it, I called my mom to share my vision.

She listened thoughtfully and attentively as she always did. And then she said, "Edie, I'd really love you to use your university degree. Yoga teachers don't make much more than professional dancers, so how do you expect to sustain a life doing that?

Please, use your university degree and do something within that profession."

So I ignored the nudges of my heart and focused on building a business "career."

By September 2016, I was working in Toronto in marketing and events. By March 2017, I'd landed what I thought was the doorway to my "dream job." I was at an international insurance brokerage on the national marketing and communications team in the Toronto office. I handled all content marketing, email marketing, thought leadership events, the creation of the corporate social responsibility program for Canada and the national rollout, as well as handling employee engagement and internal sales initiatives, which reported directly to the CEO. I also was project managing the development of a book that covered topics discussed in the summit that we hosted in October 2017. There were a lot of moving parts and I felt a lot of stress. On top of the workload, my boss and I did not see eye to eye. My hiring manager had resigned in November 2017, and we had yet to fill her spot. So it was the same workload and company expectations with less staff. My sleep was compromised and my body was screaming at me with worsening health issues to get my attention. Terrified of failure, I was locked in my head, swallowed by my job, and suppressing the messages from my heart.

Throughout all my work projects and our team changes, I always made time to be on my yoga mat and to connect with my breath and body. Whether it was fifteen minutes at home before work or a few weekly classes at a local studio, I made the time. It was my sanctuary amid the busyness of my life. And it's the "thing" that held me through all the changes that led me to where I am right now.

It was a typical Thursday in January 2018 when the magic began. At the end of a weekly yoga class with one of my favorite instructors, she shared that she was hosting a seven-day yoga and meditation retreat in Bali that April. EVERY part of my body went tingly, and I started crying. It was as if she saw my soul and was speaking directly to ME. My heart heard this call and said: "I have to go. I HAVE to go!" I'd been wanting to go on a yoga retreat or do my YTT in Bali for the past three years. I finally listened to my heart and made it happen.

The retreat was more than I imagined. It literally changed me AND my life as I knew it up to that point.

Diving into fears

That week in Bali, I dove deep into all of my shadows and fears. My instructor held me steady through it all. She knew that I could handle what I was choosing to explore—and I chose to dive heart first into everything: inner child, shadow self, inner critic, limiting beliefs, self-love, acceptance, and forgiveness. You name it, I CHOSE to get to know it that week. The retreat shattered me open, bringing me face-to-face with my heart, serving as a launch point into ALL my self-discovery work that followed.

Instead of avoiding or fearing my answers to "big" questions, all of a sudden I wanted to KNOW:

What is this bigger energy that connects and sustains all of us?

What is my purpose?

Why am I the way I am?

Who do I want to BE?

What is my relationship with my family and my family of origin?

When do I feel most present, relaxed, and alive?

What are my fears and how are they keeping me stuck?

From the retreat experience, I realized that this was just the TIP of the iceberg. It was the start of my "spiritual awakening," which was less sunshine and rainbows and more a "dark night of the soul" experience.

I realized there was more to me. More to life. More to learn, to explore, to get curious about: the rat race, the competition, the comparing, the constantly striving, my increasing stress levels, sleep issues, headaches, brain fog, sciatic pain, AND partying hard on the weekends or counting down the days till I could leave the city—that was NOT living. It was merely surviving.

I quickly realized I NEEDED to change my career path and my life. ASAP.

Being in an office tied to a computer and desk living someone else's dream drained my soul. My heart yelled at me! I KNEW that what I wanted MOST was to work with people one-on-one. I wanted to help them reconnect with their body, breath, heart, and mind. To help them feel empowered in their life, in alignment with their truth, and ALIVE within each moment.

Working in corporate, I could SEE how many people were dying inside. They would self-medicate with alcohol or more work. Stress leave and sick leave were "normal." Not handling workload with ease was viewed as a hit to someone's self-worth and overall capability. Work defined people's value instead of people defining and claiming their own life. I couldn't bear to witness it or be in that toxicity any longer. People NEEDED tools to reduce their stress and manage it in general. It became crystal clear to me that I NEEDED to help people with their well-being. The company structure was toxic because on the individual level, few people were equipped to handle stress. They needed a simple, actionable, and preventive approach to support their health and longevity. They needed to learn the secret to thriving, not just surviving.

Through this intense observation and self-reflection, I realized that I was the common piece in ALL my experiences—the awesome moments and the shitty ones—and only I could change my life for the better . . . so I DID.

In September 2018, I quit. In October I packed up my condo and moved out of the city and back in with my parents. It was terrifying and freeing. Though I had no set plan, I knew in my heart that everything was going to work out.

I was excited to be out of the city and back in nature. I was excited to dive DEEP into therapy to learn about myself, my beliefs, fears, doubts, and thought patterns. Taking ownership for our actions is scary, but it's also so empowering! Once we know something, we have the power to change it if we don't like it, and to keep doing it if we do.

During this period of transition, my intention was to live with my parents for four months: to reset (gain clarity and heal from burnout) and map out my next steps. I thought I'd attend therapy, dive deeper into my yoga practice, catch up on sleep, and head somewhere tropical to finally complete my 200-hour YTT come January 2019.

The universe had a VERY different plan.

Yes, I did go to therapy, attend daily yoga classes, and volunteer at a local yoga studio. I also took my mom to various doctor appointments and became her biggest health advocate. SHE was the reason my heart guided me home.

In October 2018, my mom started showing bizarre symptoms that became increasingly concerning. After loads of appointments and tests in the months following, we took her to Toronto General Hospital in January 2019 for more answers.

I remember the moment clearly. It was 11 a.m. on January 30. It was an extremely sunny and cold day. The doctors asked us to meet in the visitors' lounge on my mom's floor. We'd agreed to meet there instead of at her bedside if the diagnosis was fatal, so as soon as they shared the meeting location, I knew what it meant. We sat in the room in a circle. I was beside my mom holding her hand, my dad was on her other side, my sister sat beside him, and the two doctors beside her. My body was filled with feelings of fear and anxiety, so I focused on my breath. As soon as the doctors shared her diagnosis (Creutzfeldt-Jakob disease), my tears started flowing. My mom sat graciously as she received the information. She was so calm. I was stunned by the news and grateful for the way she chose to handle it, as she helped all of us fall a little bit less apart. The doctors said, "You could live for three months, six months, or one year. Because the disease is so rare, there's little data, and every case is different." I was hopeful she'd live for at least one more year.

She was with us for eight weeks.

She had six weeks at home and twelve days at hospice. Though it was quick, it was beautiful. Through her dying process and the grieving process (that accompanied and followed it), I learned the most I've ever known about love and being of service, because from the moment of her diagnosis, I again was faced with a decision: to shut down, to numb out and run, or to lean in and stay. I chose to stay. I chose to connect with my heart, bravery, vulnerability, presence, and love.

Following my intuitive nudge to quit my career and move home guided me to my mom, to myself, to my wholeness, to my purpose, and to love, AND it catapulted me to exactly where I am right now. It was an honor to be with her as she died and transitioned. As shitty and painful as it was, I got time with her. I was able to support her and shower her with love the way she did with me throughout my entire life. I also got closure on some of our disagreements, I gained a closeness with her that I'm forever grateful for, and I gained the deepest understanding of courage and love as a result of witnessing her rapid decline. My perspective on life now and my resilience and capacity to hold love is something no one can take away.

Each decision to trust the whisper in my heart required bravery:

I went from following the leader to becoming the leader and paving my own path.

I went from hating my flaws to owning my whole self.

I went from fearing death to living life more fully as a result of grief and loss.

My decision to step up and be there for my sister (and parents) in January 2015, to go to Bali and dive into self-discovery in April 2018, and to quit my job and move home in October 2018 were ALL nudges from my heart guiding me into alignment. They ultimately prepared me for my biggest "mission"—to be of service to my mom. Listening to those nudges led me to who I am now and how I guide others is closest to who I want to be as I continue evolving.

Since my mom's death, I've chosen to lean into the grief and the discomfort. I've allowed it to soften me and break me open even further. I've chosen to use my experience to help others, by sharing tools and creating environments where people can learn more about grief, processing stress and emotions, and navigating change.

Quotes I recite often are: "Everything is temporary" and "Each moment is a precious gift."

In the fall of 2019, I finally completed my 200-hour yoga teacher training.

When COVID started in March 2020, I saw it as an opportunity to step up once again by being of service to my community using the knowledge I'd gained from navigating grief on such a deep and personal level one year prior. From 2020 to 2021, my business focus evolved from stress management to burnout recovery to workplace wellness and more.

Continuing to follow the nudges of my intuition, I now empower people to navigate grief and process stress and heavy emotions with compassion and ease. Using somatic practices (movement and breathwork) and mindfulness tools, clients learn how to regulate their nervous system amid stress and discomfort, so they feel more at ease and connected in all areas of their life—regardless of how life changes around them. It is amazing, deeply fulfilling work. I am beyond grateful.

As I continue to grow, evolve, and expand in my life and business, my mission remains—to help create healthier, more inclusive, peaceful, connected, empowered, embodied, and thriving communities. I know this is just the beginning. I'm excited to see how it continues to unfold.

If you take ONE THING away from this chapter, let it be this:

Tune in to the whispers of your heart even if (and especially when) they seem extremely weird and illogical. Give them space. Listen to them. And if you begin to notice a pattern or the same message resurfacing, or if the nudge from your heart is growing stronger, give yourself permission to follow it. Allow that to be the "one decision" that you make AND notice where it takes you.

YOU are more powerful than you realize. YOU can handle the hurdles on your path. YOU hold all the answers you seek. YOU are your worst enemy and best ally. Be kind to yourself through the lows and the highs. YOU are the key to your freedom. Every experience you navigate in life is an opportunity to open, soften, and deepen your capacity for love, joy, presence, peace, and connection. Trust your heart—it knows the way.

conclusion

We all have gifts to share with this world, and while our journeys aren't the same, my goal in curating this book was to illuminate the golden threads that connect us together and the profound impact that decisions can have on our lives and businesses.

Through these pages you have witnessed how a single choice, whether momentous or seemingly inconsequential, can ignite a spark and a chain reaction of transformation, growth, and impact. And it is through peeling back the onion layers of our experiences that we find the golden threads that weave our stories together.

You are always one decision away from a totally different life.

Trust your intuition. Listen to the nudges. And follow your inner voice, even when it doesn't make any logical sense.

GOLD *nuggets*

AFFIRMATIONS FROM THE MONARCH STORIES:

Read these out loud, write them on your vision board, or create sticky notes on your desk. Speak them out into the universe and let the vibration of your voice resonate through time and space. It's amazing what can happen when you say out loud what it is you truly want.

- *It's okay to take up space.*
- *If I want things to be different, I have to make a change.*
- *I am not here to play it safe.*
- *Life is happening for me.*
- *I am living by design.*
- *I say yes before I'm ready.*
- *Investing in myself is never a waste of money.*
- *I am courageous. I am brave. I can do hard things.*
- *I surround myself with people who inspire me, who I can learn from, and who let me show up unapologetically.*
- *I am ENOUGH.*

- *I embrace the journey and chase what lights up my heart.*
- *I am not meant to be small.*
- *When I make a choice that benefits me, it's the right one, as it benefits everyone around me.*
- *I have the courage, determination, and grit to be different.*
- *I trust my intuition.*
- *Everything is temporary, and each moment is a precious gift.*
- *I am more powerful than I realize. I am the key to my freedom.*

As you close the pages of this book, we invite you to think about what your ONE thing is and to continue your own extraordinary journey of self-discovery, growth, and empowerment. Embrace the infinite potential that resides within you and allow the lessons and experiences shared in this book to guide you as you navigate the twists and turns of life.

Remember, you are capable of creating the life you desire, and every decision you make holds the power to shape and impact your journey. Embrace the possibilities ahead of you and let your journey unfold with courage, authenticity, and an unwavering commitment to your dreams. May the golden thread that connects us continue to weave its magic in your life, igniting the spark within and propelling you forward with purpose, resilience, and belief in your own power.

And with that, I want to leave you with the same final words I left you with in *The Monarch* book:

- *You are always one decision away from a totally different life.*
- *The biggest and scariest decisions always level up your life.*
- *What got you here, where you are now, won't get you to where you want to go.*
- *You are here for a reason.*
- *Trust your gut, your intuition, and your heart's guidance.*
- *You are worthy of all the success and ease that comes your way.*
- *Everyone benefits when you care for yourself.*
- *You are totally worthy and deserving of the life you dream of.*
- *Own your unique power and help others own theirs too.*
- *Do it differently.*
- *When one of us shines, we all shine.*
- *Do not dim your light. Shine bright for everyone to see!*

Amanda xo

gratitudes

TO MY COAUTHORS

My heart swells with profound gratitude and immense joy from this journey. I am filled with awe at the collective brilliance woven into these pages. Jess, Julia, Kianna, Amanda, Jodie, Nona, Lori, Caitlin, Amanda, Vanessa, and Edie, your dedication, vulnerability, and authentic voices have breathed life into this project, and I am forever grateful for the opportunity to have collaborated with each of you. Your stories, insights, and unwavering commitment to growth have left a mark, and I thank you from the bottom of my heart for trusting my vision through this process. Through your ONE DECISION to say HECK YES to yourselves, your visions, to me as your guide through this author journey, you have not only impacted your own lives, but you have become beacons of inspiration for others.

Each of you has contributed a unique thread to the tapestry of our collective narrative, a thread that has transformed this book into something truly extraordinary. In the spirit of our shared journey, I want to extend my deepest gratitude for the trust you have placed in me and for allowing your voices to be heard within these pages. Your vulnerability and authenticity have created a safe space for readers to connect, learn, and grow. I am honored to have been entrusted with your stories and to have played a role in bringing them to light and flight. And like a stage mom behind the scenes, I am cheering you on every step of the way and am so proud of who you are being in this world. Keep rocking your badass selves and shining bright for everyone to see!

TO THE SOUL SEED TEAM

Thank you for helping us birth this book into the world. Your guidance, patience, professionalism, and hearts helped this journey be the magic that it was. Thank you for doing what you do in this world, so that we can make a bigger impact with the work we do.

TO OUR FAMILIES, FRIENDS, COACHES, AND TEAMS

Thank you for your support, love, and guidance through this journey. The journey to become an author has a profound impact on the writer and those who are in their orbit. The writing process is a journey that can break you open in ways you can't prepare for and having the love, support, and guidance from family, friends, coaches, and your team through the process is life-giving.

TO OUR READERS, CUSTOMERS, STUDENTS, AND CLIENTS

Thank you for listening to your intuition and making this one decision to pick up and journey through this book. Thank you for your support in purchasing this book, our offers and services, and by helping spread the word for others to enjoy and experience. Without your support, we wouldn't be able to do what we do in this world. It is an honor to be a part of your journey, and we look forward to continuing to support you in reaching your goals, achieving your dreams, and embracing your fullest potential.

TO THE MONARCH COMMUNITY

Thank you for being the source of inspiration. It is an honor to serve a community of heart-centered individuals who support and uplift one another. Your presence, engagement, and support have made all the difference—and I am truly grateful for the opportunity to serve you.

CONTINUE THE MOMENTUM:

I hope the words on these pages from fellow Monarchs inspired, motivated, and encouraged you along your journey. If you are a woman entrepreneur who is starting or growing your business, we would love to invite you to join the Monarch Community—a space where heart-centered women entrepreneurs thrive! The community is absolutely incredible, supportive, and inspiring. You can find out more here: *https://www.themonarchandco. com/Monarch-Momentum*

If you enjoyed this book and the stories inside, you may also enjoy my first book, the best-selling *The Monarch: The Signature 8 Method for Launching Your Dream Business with Clarity, Confidence, and Love*. You can visit here for a copy: *https://www.themonarchandco.com/book*

And if you're looking for clarity and a roadmap, let's connect! I love meeting and helping heart-centered entrepreneurs who are looking to make a positive impact on this world. You can email me at amanda@themonarchandco.com or book a free connection call with me here: *https://www.themonarchandco.com/*

I look forward to connecting with you again soon!

Amanda

RECOMMENDED RESOURCES AND WORKS CITED

Introduction

Sharon Blackie. *If Women Rose Rooted*. September Publishing, 2019.

Chapter 1

Chris Buck and Jennifer Lee. *Frozen II*. Disney, 2019.

Tara Swart. *The Source: The Secrets of the Universe, the Science of the Brain*. HarperAudio, 2019.

Jenna Zoe's Human Design app: https://www.myhumandesignapp.com/

Chapter 5

Adele Tevlin podcast: https://podcasts.apple.com/us/podcast/coffee-conversations-with-adele-tevlin/id1567212095

Brené Brown. *Rising Strong: The Reckoning. The Rumble. The Revolution*. Random House, 2015.

Chapter 7

B.K.S. Iyengar. *Light on Life: The Yoga Journey to Wholeness, Inner Peace, and Ultimate Freedom*. Rodale Books, 2005.

Lewis Carroll. *Alice's Adventures in Wonderland*. Macmillan, 1865.

SOUL SEED
LEGACY · HOUSE

At Soul Seed Legacy House, we help thought leaders and creative entrepreneurs capture their vision in the form of nonfiction books, journals, workbooks, affirmation cards, and personal growth products.

Our mission is to help our authors grow and scale a platform far beyond the book, protect their soul's work, and turn their message into a legacy!

www.sslegacyhouse.com

 @sslegacyhouse

www.ingramcontent.com/pod-product-compliance
Lightning Source LLC
Chambersburg PA
CBHW051312120626
46547CB00015B/2198